Wonderful ways to prepare

LAMB

by **MARION MANSFIELD**

STUFFED LAMB CUTLETS (RECIPE PAGE 17)

Wonderful ways to prepare
LAMB

H.C. PUBLISHING INC.
FLORIDA, USA

COVER PICTURE — LEG OF LAMB WITH BEANS (RECIPE PAGE 24)

FIRST PUBLISHED 1984
FIRST U.S. EDITION 1984

PUBLISHED AND COPYRIGHT © 1984
BY AYERS & JAMES
CROWS NEST, N.S.W., AUSTRALIA

DISTRIBUTED BY
AYERS & JAMES, CROWS NEST, N.S.W., AUSTRALIA
H.C. PUBLISHING INC., U.S.A.

PRINTED IN SINGAPORE
HARD COVER EDITION: ISBN 0 87637 929 3
SOFT COVER EDITION: ISBN 0 87637 941 2

TITLES AVAILABLE IN THIS SERIES: BEEF,
FISH & SEAFOOD, POULTRY, STEWS & CASSEROLES,
BARBECUES & PICNIC MEALS, CHINESE MEALS,
SALADS, SOUPS, ITALIAN MEALS, LAMB,
CAKES & COOKIES, DESSERTS.

SPANISH LAMB WITH STUFFED
ONION RINGS (RECIPE PAGE 20) ▶

◀ OVERLEAF — MARINATED LEG OF HOGGET (RECIPE PAGE 20)

Noisettes with Tomatoes and Beans

Serves: 4
Cooking time: 25–30 minutes

4 lamb loin chops
4 tablespoons butter
salt and pepper
1 lb (500 g) French beans, trimmed
boiling salted water
2 large tomatoes, cut in half
4 hamburger buns, sliced in half
parsley for garnish

Have your butcher trim the chops and form into noisettes. Melt half the butter in a large pan, add noisettes and brown on each side over high heat.

Reduce heat and sprinkle meat with salt and pepper, cover and cook over low heat for 8–10 minutes. Uncover and cook a further 6–8 minutes, then lift out to a dish and keep warm. Meanwhile, cook beans in a pan of boiling salted water for 10–12 minutes until tender but crisp, drain well, add 2 teaspoons butter, salt and pepper, cover and keep warm.

Add remaining butter to pan juices and heat, add tomato halves, cut side down and sear over high heat for 3–4 minutes. Lift out tomatoes and place each half on a half a bun, place noisettes on remaining bun halves and serve with the beans. Garnish with parsley.

LAMB CHOPS ON RICED POTATOES (RECIPE PAGE 21) ▶

Ragout of Beans and Lamb

Serves: 4
Cooking time: 1¼ hours

3 tablespoons butter
1 lb (500 g) lamb neck chops
2 scallions, chopped
1 medium onion, chopped
2 medium carrots, thinly sliced
2 medium carrots, cut in large pieces
2 sprigs parsley
salt and pepper
½ teaspoon oregano
a bouquet garni
1 cup (250 ml) Basic Bouillon — see recipe
    page 89
½ lb (250 g) white haricot beans, cooked and
    drained

Melt butter in a flameproof casserole, add chops and cook over moderate heat until brown on all sides, add scallions, onion, all the carrots, parsley, salt, pepper, oregano, a bouquet garni of thyme, bay leaf and basil and bouillon. Cover and cook over moderately low heat for 30 minutes, add the beans, cover and cook over low heat a further 35–40 minutes. Discard bouquet garni, and serve with crusty bread.

Garlic Lamb and Beans

Serves: 4
Cooking time: 1¼ hours

4 tablespoons oil
1½ lbs (750 g) lean lamb, cubed
2 heads of garlic, separated into cloves and
    peeled
1 teaspoon finely chopped thyme
½ teaspoon ground bay leaves
½ teaspoon salt
1 cup (250 ml) Beef Stock — see recipe
    page 90
1 lb (500 g) French beans, trimmed and sliced
boiling salted water
toasted bread slices

Heat oil in a large pan, add lamb and cook over high heat to brown on all sides, reduce heat and add garlic cloves, thyme, ground bay leaves, salt and stock, cover and simmer over low heat for 45 minutes. Remove cover and simmer a further 16–20 minutes.

Meanwhile, cook beans in a pan of boiling salted water for 10–12 minutes and drain. Add to the pan and stir to cover with pan juices, then serve with toasted bread slices.

▼

SADDLE OF LAMB CHOPS (RECIPE PAGE 17) ▶

Crown Roast of Lamb

Serves: 6
Cooking time: 1¼–1½ hours
Oven: 180°C 350°F

1 lamb crown
6 tablespoons butter
salt and pepper
12 small tomatoes
1½ lbs (750 g) French beans, trimmed
boiling salted water
1½ tablespoons flour
1 tablespoon finely chopped fresh mint
1 cup (250 ml) Beef Stock — see recipe
  page 90
½ cup (125 ml) white wine
six baked potatoes

Have your butcher prepare and form the crown from 2 racks, each of 6 ribs or 2 best ends of neck and trim the bones clean 1″ (2½ cm) from the tips. Cover the bone tips with foil, brush the crown with 4 tablespoons melted butter and sprinkle with salt and pepper. Place in a baking pan and cook in a moderate oven for 1¼–1½ hours or until tender. Meanwhile, trim the tomatoes and brush with 2 teaspoons butter, place around the crown and cook for 20–25 minutes. Cook beans in a pan of boiling salted water for 10–12 minutes or until tender but crisp, drain, add remaining butter, salt and pepper, cover and keep warm.

Spoon beans on to a serving dish, lift out the crown and place on the beans, replace foil with paper frills, add tomatoes around the meat and keep warm. Pour most of the fat from the pan, add flour, salt, pepper and mint and stir over heat to lightly brown. Add stock and heat, stirring and scraping to deglaze the pan, stir in wine and bring to the boil, stirring constantly, into a smooth sauce, then pour into a sauce dish and serve with the crown roast, together with baked potatoes.

STUFFED LAMB HINDQUARTER, HOT OR COLD (RECIPE PAGE 24) ▶

Lamb Chops with Prunes and Raisins

Serves: 4
Cooking time: 1¼ hours

2 cups pitted prunes
1½ cups seedless raisins
water
3 tablespoons butter
1 tablespoon oil
1½ lbs (750 g) lamb or mutton shoulder
  chops
½ teaspoon saffron
2 teaspoons cinnamon
½ teaspoon salt
small pinch of black pepper
4 cloves garlic, crushed
1 tablespoon brown sugar
2 cups (500 ml) water
1 cup (250 ml) orange juice

Soak prunes and raisins in a bowl of water for 2 hours to plump, then drain. Heat butter and oil in a flameproof casserole, add chops and cook until brown on each side. Add saffron, cinnamon, salt, black pepper and garlic and stir, cover and cook over moderately low heat for 15 minutes. Mix brown sugar in a bowl with water and orange juice and stir to dissolve sugar, add to the meat, stir and bring to simmering point, cover and simmer for 15 minutes. Add prunes and raisins, half cover, cook a further 30 minutes and serve.

    BARBECUED CHOPS IN TARRAGON (RECIPE PAGE 21) ▶

Mutton Hash with Poached Eggs

Serves: 4
Cooking time: 35–40 minutes
Oven: 180°C 350°F

4 tablespoons butter
1 medium onion, chopped
1 clove garlic, crushed
½ small red bell pepper, finely chopped
2 large tomatoes, peeled and chopped
1½ lbs (750 g) leftover cooked mutton,
  diced
2 large potatoes, cooked and diced
¾ cup (185 ml) tomato purée
good pinch of nutmeg
salt and pepper
½ lb (250 g) shelled peas
boiling salted water
2 cups (500 ml) water
1 teaspoon salt
1 teaspoon malt vinegar
4 eggs

Melt butter in a large pan, add onion and sauté 2–3 minutes, add garlic, red pepper and tomatoes and cook 8–10 minutes, stirring and mashing. Add diced meat, potatoes, tomato purée, nutmeg, salt and pepper to taste and stir. Pour into an ovenproof casserole dish, cover tightly and cook in a moderate oven for 20–25 minutes.

Meanwhile, cook peas in a pan of boiling salted water for 10–12 minutes, drain and keep warm. Heat water in a pan with salt and vinegar until boiling, then reduce heat. Break eggs, one at a time, into a small bowl, then slide into the liquid and simmer for 3 minutes or until egg whites are set. Spoon the hash onto a warm dish and add peas, lift out eggs with a slotted spoon and place on the dish, then serve.

PARSLEY COATED LAMB WITH BEANS (RECIPE PAGE 25) ▶

Lamb Shoulder with Prunes

Serves: 4
Cooking time: 50–60 minutes
Oven: 230°C reduced to 180°C
450°F reduced to 350°F

¾ lb (375 g) pitted prunes
hot water
½ cup (125 ml) white wine
⅔ cup (165 ml) Beef Stock — see recipe
   page 90
2 lbs (1 kg) boned shoulder of lamb
3 tablespoons melted butter
salt and pepper
1 teaspoon thyme
1 bay leaf
4 medium carrots, cut into pieces
salted water
2 teaspoons extra butter
1 lb (500 g) green peas, shelled
8 small onions, peeled

stock, bring to simmering point and simmer for 10 minutes. Strain the liquid into a bowl and reserve, and keep prunes warm.
Trim the lamb, roll and tie securely with string, place on a rack in a baking pan and brush with melted butter on all sides. Cook in a very hot oven for 15 minutes, reduce heat to moderate, sprinkle meat with salt, pepper and thyme and add bay leaf to the pan. Cook for 15 minutes, then pour reserved prune stock over the meat and cook a further 15 minutes for rare, 20–25 minutes for well done. Lift out meat to a warm dish and allow to rest for 10 minutes. Heat pan juices, stirring and scraping to deglaze the pan, then pour into a sauce dish and keep warm.
Meanwhile, bring carrots to the boil in a pan of salted water, cook for 12–15 minutes and drain, add 1 teaspoon butter, salt and pepper, cover and keep warm. Cook peas and onions in a pan of boiling salted water for 10–12 minutes, drain and add remaining 1 teaspoon butter, salt and pepper. Serve the lamb, carved into slices with sauce, prunes, carrots, peas and onions.

Soak the prunes in a bowl of hot water to cover for 1 hour and drain, then place in a pan, add wine and

Stuffed Lamb Cutlets

Serves: 4–6
Cooking time: 20–25 minutes

6 lamb cutlets
1 egg, beaten with 2 teaspoons water
fine dry breadcrumbs
3 tablespoons butter
1 tablespoon oil
sprigs of parsley

Stuffing:
1½ cups ground, cooked chicken meat
2 slices ham, ground
¼ lb (125 g) mushrooms, minced
salt and pepper
1 cup (250 ml) Béchamel Sauce — see recipe
  page 92

For the stuffing, combine all ingredients in a bowl and mix well. Trim the cutlets and lightly pound with a meat mallet, spread stuffing mixture over the cutlets, firming well, dip in egg and coat well with breadcrumbs. Heat butter and oil in a large pan until hot, add cutlets, sear to seal, then cook over moderately low heat for 20–25 minutes, turning often, until golden brown. Drain on paper towels and serve garnished with sprigs of parsley.
(Illustrated on page 1.)

Saddle of Lamb Chops

Serves: 4
Cooking time: 35–40 minutes

1½ lbs (750 g) saddle of lamb
2 large carrots, diced
2 large potatoes, peeled and diced
salted water
8 tablespoons butter
salt and pepper
½ bunch spinach, trimmed and chopped
1 teaspoon salt
½ teaspoon nutmeg
10–12 spring onions, trimmed to bulbs only
¼ lb (125 g) button mushrooms

Have your butcher cut the saddle into 4 slices. Cook carrots and potatoes together in a pan of salted water for 15 minutes or until soft, drain well, and mash to a purée, add 3 teaspoons butter, salt and pepper and mix well, cover and keep warm. Wash the spinach in a colander, shake off excess water and place in a pan with 1 teaspoon salt, cover and cook for 6–8 minutes, or until limp, drain well and add 2 teaspoons butter, salt, pepper and nutmeg, stir, cover and keep warm.
Meanwhile, melt 3 tablespoons butter in a large pan, add lamb and cook over moderate heat for 8–10 minutes to brown on each side. Reduce heat, cover and cook a further 18–20 minutes or until tender, then lift out to a dish and keep warm.
Melt remaining butter in a pan, add spring onions and sauté over moderate heat until golden brown, lift out and place with the lamb. To pan juices add mushrooms and sauté 5–6 minutes, remove and place beside the meat, then serve with spinach and potato-carrot purée.
(Illustrated on page 9.)

Creamed Sweetbreads on Rice

Serves: 4
Cooking time: 3–4 minutes

1 lb (500 g) Sweetbreads — see recipe page 46
1½ cups (375 ml) hot Béchamel Sauce — see
  recipe page 92
hot cooked rice
paprika
finely chopped parsley

Cut the drained sweetbreads into cubes and add to a pan of hot béchamel sauce, heat, but do not boil, then pour into a rice ring, dust with paprika and chopped parsley and serve.

Grilled Stuffed Cutlets

Serves: 4–6
Cooking time: 20–25 minutes

8 thick lamb cutlets
8 slices bacon
Herb Baste — see recipe page 91
2 cups freshly shelled Lima beans
boiling salted water
1 tablespoon butter
salt and pepper
sprigs of parsley

Stuffing:
3 tablespoons butter
1 small onion, minced
¼ lb (125 g) sausage meat
salt and pepper
½ teaspoon thyme
⅛ teaspoon ground bay leaves
1 clove garlic, crushed
¼ lb (125 g) mushrooms, finely chopped
1 egg

For the stuffing, melt butter in a pan, add onion and sauté 2–3 minutes, add sausage meat and cook over moderate heat for 4–5 minutes, stirring, until lightly browned. Remove pan from heat, sprinkle with salt, pepper, thyme, ground bay leaves, stir in garlic, mushrooms and egg and mix well.
Divide stuffing into 8 portions, spread on the cutlets and wrap with bacon slices. Thread two cutlets on each skewer and place on a rack 4″–6″ (10–15 cm) from heat and grill for 20–25 minutes, turning often and brushing with the baste.
Meanwhile, cook beans in a pan of boiling salted water for 10–12 minutes and drain, add butter, salt and pepper, serve with the cutlets and garnish with parsley sprigs.

CUTLETS IN TARRAGON CREAM SAUCE (RECIPE PAGE 25) ▶

Braised Onions

Serves: 2–4
Cooking time: 30–35 minutes

2 teaspoons butter
3 teaspoons oil
16–18 pearl onions, peeled
½ cup (125 ml) Beef Stock — see recipe
*   page 90*
salt and pepper
a bouquet garni

Heat butter and oil in a pan, add onions and baste, cover and cook over moderately low heat for 8–10 minutes, shaking the pan often, until onions are browned. Stir in stock, salt and pepper to taste and add a bouquet garni of thyme, bay leaf and parsley. Cover and simmer gently for 20–25 minutes, discard bouquet garni and serve to accompany a dish for 2, or keep warm to add to a dish for 4.

Marinated Leg of Lamb

Serves: 6–8
Cooking time: 2–2¼ hours
Oven: 230°C reduced to 180°C
        450°F reduced to 350°F

4 lbs (2 kg) lean leg of lamb
3 tablespoons oil
3 cloves garlic, crushed
salt and pepper
pinch of ground juniper berries
½ teaspoon thyme
1 teaspoon ground bay leaves
1 tablespoon finely chopped parsley
5 small carrots, thinly sliced
5 small onions, thinly sliced
¼ cup red wine
½ cup Beef Stock — see recipe page 90
2 tablespoons brandy
1 tablespoon red currant jam, sieved

Trim the leg and place in a deep glass or enamel dish. Heat oil in a pan, add garlic, salt, pepper, ground juniper berries, thyme, ground bay leaves and parsley and cook, stirring, for 1–2 minutes. Add carrots and onions, cover and cook over moderate heat for 5–6 minutes, shaking pan often. Stir in wine and stock, bring to simmering point and simmer 3–4 minutes, remove pan from heat and cool, then pour over the meat. Cover and place in the refrigerator to marinate for 24 hours, turning and basting occasionally. Lift out meat and place in a baking pan and cook in a very hot oven for 15 minutes to brown. Reduce heat to moderate, pour marinade over the meat and cook for 1¼ hours. Pour brandy over the leg and cook a further 10–12 minutes or until meat is tender. Lift out meat to a warm dish and allow to rest for 10 minutes in a warm place. Scrape to deglaze pan over heat, stir in currant jam until mixed, then put through a blender, return to a pan, heat and pour into a sauce dish. Carve the leg of lamb and serve with the sauce.
(Illustrated on pages 2 & 3.)

Spanish Lamb with Stuffed Onion Rings

Serves: 4
Cooking time: 35–40 minutes
Oven: 160°C   325°F

4 tablespoons olive oil
4 thick lamb chops
salt and pepper
4 slices of ham
½ cup white wine
¾ cup Beef Stock — see recipe page 90
3 medium white onions, thickly sliced
boiling water
4 tablespoons butter
2 medium onions, chopped
2 large tomatoes, peeled and chopped
½ cup blanched almonds
3 tablespoons grated, unsweetened chocolate
1 teaspoon ground cloves
1 teaspoon ground cinnamon
2 teaspoons gelatin

Heat oil in a large pan, add chops and sear to brown on each side, transfer to an ovenproof casserole, but reserve pan juices. Sprinkle with salt and pepper, place a slice of ham on each chop, sprinkle with half the wine and ½ cup of stock, cover and cook in a moderately slow oven for 30—35 minutes.

Meanwhile, place thick onion slices in a bowl of boiling water for 2—3 minutes, drain well and separate into rings. To reserved pan juices add half the butter and melt, add chopped onions and sauté until transparent, add tomatoes and cook 3—4 minutes, stirring and mashing to pulp. Cover and cook over very low heat for 8—10 minutes.

Melt remaining butter in a pan, add almonds and cook until browned, stir in grated chocolate, cloves and cinnamon and cook, stirring, to coat the almonds, then lift out and set aside, stir remaining wine into the pan, bring to simmering point and simmer 2—3 minutes. Heat remaining stock, add gelatin and stir to dissolve, then stir into the pan and simmer 2—3 minutes for a sauce.

Place ham topped chops on a dish and sprinkle with almonds, arrange onion rings around the meat and fill with tomato and onion mixture, spoon sauce around the meat and serve.

(Illustrated on page 5.)

Lamb Chops on Riced Potatoes

Serves: 4
Cooking time: 10—12 minutes

8 thick rib loin chops
Herb Baste — see recipe page 91
2 large potatoes, peeled and chopped
boiling salted water
1 tablespoon finely chopped parsley
2 teaspoons finely chopped chervil
1 clove garlic, crushed
salt and pepper
1 egg, lightly beaten
3 tablespoons butter
4 small tomatoes
Fresh Relish — see recipe page 86

Place chops on a rack 4" (10 cm) from heat and broil 2 minutes each side, brush with the baste and cook a further 6—8 minutes, turning and basting often, then keep warm.

Meanwhile, cook potatoes in a pan of boiling salted water for 3 minutes and drain well, put through a ricer or coarse sieve into a bowl. Add parsley, chervil, garlic, salt, pepper and egg and lightly mix. Heat butter in a large pan, spread potato mixture over the pan base and cook over high heat until golden brown. Divide into 4 portions and place on warm serving dishes, add 2 chops and 1 tomato to each dish and serve with suggested relish, a green salad, crusty bread and red wine.

(Illustrated on page 7.)

Barbecued Chops in Tarragon

Serves: 4
Cooking time: 12—15 minutes
Barbecue on the grid over medium hot coals

4 tablespoons softened butter
4 tablespoons finely chopped tarragon
6 tablespoons oil
1 tablespoon lemon juice
8 loin chops
salt and pepper
8 egg tomatoes, halved lengthways

Mix softened butter in a bowl with half the tarragon until blended, then chill. Mix oil, lemon juice and remaining tarragon in a jar, cover and shake briskly until fully blended, for a baste. Trim the chops and brush with the baste on each side, then set aside in a glass dish for 30 minutes. Brush chops again and sprinkle with salt and pepper, place on the grill over medium hot coals and cook for 12—15 minutes or until tender, turning and basting often.

Place tomatoes on the grill, cut side up and cook for 3 minutes, brush with the baste, turn and cook a further 3—4 minutes to brown. Spoon a little tarragon butter on each chop and serve with the tomatoes.

(Illustrated on page 13.)

▲ SPINACH STUFFED LAMB FOREQUARTER (RECIPE PAGE 28)

▲ KIDNEY STUFFED WHOLE LOIN (RECIPE PAGE 28)

Boiled Mutton with Caper Sauce

Serves: 8–10
Cooking time: 2¼–2½ hours

6–7 lbs (3 kg) leg of young mutton
2 teaspoons salt
boiling water to cover
10–12 small carrots, scraped
6 leeks, trimmed
10–12 small new potatoes

Caper Sauce:
3 tablespoons butter, melted
3 tablespoons flour
2 cups (500 ml) boiling Vegetable Stock — see
*   recipe page 90*
1 egg yolk
3 tablespoons cream
salt and pepper
1 tablespoon lemon juice
2 tablespoons finely chopped capers
4 tablespoons extra butter
finely chopped parsley

Trim all but a thin layer of fat from the leg, discarding any loose fat. Add salt to a large, deep pan of boiling water and stir, add the leg and return liquid to simmering point. Cover and simmer gently over low heat for 1 hour, add carrots, leeks and potatoes and simmer a further 1–1¼ hours or until meat is tender.

Meanwhile, for the sauce, mix melted butter and flour in a pan until a smooth paste, pour in boiling stock and whisk briskly until blended. Beat egg yolk and cream together in a bowl and, still beating, add ½ cup of the sauce, drop by drop, then add remaining sauce in a thin stream and beat vigorously. Pour mixture back into the pan and bring quickly to the boil, beating constantly, and boil for one minute, remove pan from heat, add salt, pepper, lemon juice and capers and mix well. Add extra butter in small pieces and beat until fully blended, then pour sauce into a serving bowl and sprinkle with chopped parsley. Lift out the leg, carve and serve with the vegetables and caper sauce.

Leg of Lamb with Beans

Serves: 6–8
Cooking time: 1½–1¾ hours
Oven: 230°C reduced to 180°C
        450°F reduced to 350°F

4 lbs (2 kg) leg of lamb
2 cloves garlic, slivered
3 tablespoons margarine, melted
1 tablespoon oil
1 medium onion, chopped
1 medium carrot, chopped
salt and pepper
1 cup (250 ml) stock
½ lb (250 g) French beans, trimmed
boiling salted water
nob of butter or margarine
2 tablespoons butter
¼ lb (125 g) simmered and drained haricot
  beans
1 clove garlic, crushed
1 tablespoon lemon juice
chopped parsley
2 medium tomatoes, quartered

Trim the leg of lamb and insert garlic slivers, brush with a mixture of melted margarine and oil and place on a rack in a baking pan. Cook in a hot oven for 15 minutes to sear and brown, turning once and basting with margarine-oil mixture. Reduce heat to moderate, add onion and carrot to the base of the pan, under the rack, and cook for 1–1¼ hours. Sprinkle meat with salt and pepper, lift onto a hot dish and allow to rest for 15–20 minutes, but keep warm. Remove rack and spoon fat from the pan. Stir in stock and cook over high heat, mashing and scraping to deglaze the pan. Sprinkle with salt and pepper to taste, strain into a gravy bowl and keep hot.
Meanwhile cook French beans in a pan of boiling salted water for 10–12 minutes and drain, add nob of butter or margarine, salt and pepper and keep hot. Melt butter in a pan, add drained haricot beans and crushed garlic, heat, shaking pan to mix, for 5–6 minutes, stir in lemon juice, cover and keep warm. Place a frill on the bone of the leg and arrange French and haricot beans on the dish.

Sprinkle with chopped parsley, garnish with tomato quarters and serve.
(Illustrated on front cover & page 4.)

Stuffed Lamb Hindquarter, Hot or Cold

Serves: 8
Cooking time: 2–2¼ hours
Oven: 230°C reduced to 180°C
        450°F reduced to 350°F

6–7 lbs (3 kg) hindquarter of lamb
3 cups soft breadcrumbs
⅓ cup milk
4 cloves garlic, crushed
4 scallions, white only, finely chopped or minced
salt and pepper
1 egg
1 tablespoon finely chopped parsley
2 extra cloves garlic, slivered
4 tablespoons butter, melted
⅓ cup (85 ml) dry white wine
4 tablespoons water
1 cup (250 ml) Hot Water Mayonnaise — see
  recipe page 91
1 teaspoon chopped mint
1 tablespoon finely chopped parsley
tomato wedges

Have your butcher cut out the chine, tail, pelvic, rump knuckle and leg bones from the hind-quarter, leaving the shank bone intact. Open out the meat and lay on a board, skin side down. Soak bread-crumbs in milk, then squeeze out most of the liquid, combine crumbs with crushed garlic, scallions, salt, pepper, egg and parsley and mix well. Spread the stuffing on the meat, roll lamb firmly and fasten with skewers or tie securely with string. Cut incisions at the shank end, insert garlic slivers and brush meat

with melted butter. Place lamb in a baking pan and cook in a very hot oven for 15 minutes to seal and brown, reduce heat to moderate and cook for 1¾ hours for rare, 2 hours for well done. Lift out lamb, place on a carving dish and allow to rest for 10 minutes to set the meat. Pour off fat from the pan, add wine and water and heat, stirring and scraping to deglaze the pan, pour ¼ cup into a small bowl and reserve. Thicken remaining liquid with a gravy mix and cook 2–3 minutes, then pour into a sauce dish. Carve the lamb and serve hot with the sauce. Allow remaining meat to cool, then wrap and chill. Stir reserved pan liquid into mayonnaise, add mint and mix until blended, sprinkle with parsley and chill. Carve cold meat and serve with tomato wedges and mayonnaise for a second meal.
(Illustrated on page 11.)

together in a bowl, melt 1 tablespoon butter and add to the mixture with warm water and mix until blended. Spread the mixture over the lamb and cook a further 15–20 minutes.

Meanwhile, cook beans in boiling salted water for 10–12 minutes or until tender. Drain, reserving liquid, and place in a bowl and keep warm. Melt remaining butter in a pan, add onion and sauté until golden, add bouillon and stir in wine, stock and ½ cup reserved liquid. Bring to the boil and boil over high heat to reduce liquid by half, then pour over the beans and serve with the lamb, sprinkled with parsley.
(Illustrated on page 15.)

Parsley Coated Lamb with Beans

Serves: 4–6
Cooking time: 1½–1¾ hours
Oven: 180°C 350°F

3 lbs (1½ kg) leg of lamb
2 cloves garlic, slivered
6 tablespoons butter
2 cloves garlic, crushed
¼ cup fine dry breadcrumbs
4 tablespoons finely chopped parsley
½ teaspoon salt
3 teaspoons warm water
2 cups freshly shelled lima beans
2 cups (500 ml) boiling salted water
1 medium onion, minced
1 bouillon cube
¼ cup white wine
¼ cup Beef Stock — see recipe page 90
extra finely chopped parsley

Cut incisions in the lamb and insert garlic slivers, melt 2 tablespoons of butter and brush over the meat. Place the lamb in a baking pan and cook in a moderate oven for 1¼ hours, turning twice. Mix crushed garlic, breadcrumbs, parsley and salt

Cutlets in Tarragon Cream Sauce

Serves: 6
Cooking time: 35–40 minutes

6 rib loin cutlets
3 tablespoons butter
½ cup (125 ml) dry white wine
juice of ½ lemon
salt and pepper
2 tablespoons finely chopped fresh tarragon
⅓ cup heavy cream

Trim the cutlets. Melt butter in a large pan, add cutlets and cook over moderate heat to brown on each side, lift out and set aside. Add wine to the pan and heat, stirring and scraping to deglaze the pan. Stir in lemon juice, salt, pepper and tarragon and bring to the boil. Reduce heat and return cutlets, cover and cook over low heat for 18–20 minutes, stir in cream and heat, but do not boil, then serve.
(Illustrated on page 19.)

Lamb Coated with Roquefort Cheese

Serves: 6–8
Cooking time: 1¾–2 hours
Oven: 230°C reduced to 180°C
450°F reduced to 350°F

4 lbs (2 kg) lean leg of lamb
6 oz (185 g) Roquefort cheese, crumbled
½ teaspoon salt
¼ teaspoon ground black pepper
2 teaspoons brandy
2 small carrots, sliced
1 teaspoon thyme
2 bay leaves
3 tablespoons white wine
2 tablespoons water
Sautéed Potatoes — see recipe page 35

Trim and lamb and wipe with a damp cloth. Mix crumbled cheese with salt, black pepper and brandy and spread over the meat in a thick coating, wrap the meat in plastic and chill for 2 hours. Combine carrots, thyme, bay leaves, wine and water in a baking pan, carefully discard plastic from the lamb and place meat on a rack in the pan. Cook in a very hot oven for 15 minutes, reduce heat to moderate and cook a further 1¼–1½ hours. Lift out the lamb to a carving dish and allow to rest for 10 minutes in a warm place, push the carrots and liquid through a fine sieve into a sauce dish. Carve the leg of lamb and serve with sautéed potatoes and the sauce.

26   CASSEROLE OF MEAT BALLS AND VEGETABLES (RECIPE PAGE 29) ▶

Kidney Stuffed Whole Loin

Serves: 6–8
Cooking time: 1–1¼ hours
Oven: 230°C reduced to 180°C
       450°F reduced to 350°F

4½–5 lbs (2¼–2½ kg) whole mid and rib loin of
   lamb
4 tablespoons melted butter
salt and pepper
½ cup (125 ml) dry white wine
2 teaspoons finely chopped fresh mint
1 cup (250 ml) Beef Stock — see recipe page 90
2 large tomatoes, cut in half
Baked Potato Nests — see recipe page 47
1 lb (500 g) cooked French beans
Sautéed Vegetables — see recipe page 50
truffles (optional)

Stuffing:
2 sheep's kidneys, trimmed and finely chopped
¼ lb (125 g) mushrooms, finely chopped
6 spring onions, white only, finely chopped
1 cup soft breadcrumbs
salt and seasoned pepper
1 tablespoon finely chopped fresh mint
¼ cup water
¼ cup dry white wine

For the stuffing combine all ingredients in a bowl and mix well.

Have your butcher trim the rib bones to loosen from the flesh and cut slits in the meat to thread the bones, then saw the chine bone to separate loin into 10. Lay the loin on a board, skin side down and spread with ¾ of the stuffing, roll the meat, inserting rib bones through slits provided and skewer to fasten. Place in a baking pan, brush with melted butter and cook in a very hot oven for 15 minutes to seal and brown the lamb, then reduce heat and cook for 30 minutes. Sprinkle with salt and pepper, and ¼ cup wine and cook a further 15–20 minutes until tender. Remove meat to a dish and allow to rest for 10 minutes in a warm place.

Pour off most of the fat from the pan, mix mint with the stock and stir into the pan, heat, stirring and scraping to deglaze the pan, stir in remaining wine and bring to the boil, thicken if necessary with gravy mix, simmer 2–3 minutes, then pour into a sauce dish and keep warm.

Meanwhile, scoop most of the flesh from the tomato halves and mix with the remaining stuffing, spoon mixture into tomato shells, place on a baking tray and cook in a moderate oven for 15–18 minutes. Then place around the meat with potato nests, French beans and sautéed vegetables. Decorate with truffle slices and serve with the sauce. (Illustrated on page 22.)

Spinach Stuffed Lamb Forequarter

Serves: 8
Cooking time: 2–2¼ hours
Oven: 230°C reduced to 180°C
       450°F reduced to 350°F

6–7 lbs (3 kg) boned forequarter of lamb
⅓ cup melted butter
4 medium carrots, cut in pieces
1 cup (250 ml) Beef Stock — see recipe page 90
½ cup (125 ml) dry white wine
4 medium tomatoes
2 large potatoes, peeled and chopped
salted water
1 spinach leaf, minced
1 tablespoon minced parsley

Stuffing:
2 cups minced spinach
¼ lb (125 g) lean ham, ground
1 cup soft breadcrumbs
3 tablespoons minced sorrel
2 tablespoons minced parsley
2 scallions, white only, minced
½ teaspoon chervil
½ teaspoon tarragon
4 tablespoons melted butter
salt and pepper

For the stuffing, combine all ingredients in a bowl and mix well. Trim the lamb and lay on a board, skin side down, spread stuffing thickly over the meat and roll firmly, but not tightly, and fasten with skewers. Brush 3 tablespoons of melted butter over the lamb, place in a baking pan and cook in a very hot oven for 15 minutes to seal and brown. Reduce oven to moderate and cook for 30 minutes, arrange carrot pieces around the meat and cook a further 30 minutes. Lift out carrot pieces, place in a warm dish and keep warm. Pour stock and wine over the meat and cook for 30 minutes, then baste with pan juices.

Place tomato halves on a rack in the oven and cook for 15−20 minutes, then remove to a dish and keep warm, lift out meat, place on a warm carving dish and allow to rest for 10 minutes. Deglaze the pan over heat by stirring and scraping, simmer for 2−3 minutes, then pour into a sauce dish and keep warm.

Meanwhile, cook potatoes in a pan of salted water with spinach and parsley for 10−12 minutes or until soft and drain, mash well with remaining butter, then heap on top of tomato halves and serve with lamb, sauce and carrots.
(Illustrated on page 22.)

Brains in Béchamel Sauce

Serves: 4
Cooking time: 25−30 minutes

4 sets of lamb's brains
cold water
3 cups (750 ml) water
1 teaspoon salt
1 small onion, stuck with 3 cloves
2 tablespoons malt vinegar
6 peppercorns, bruised
a bouquet garni
Béchamel Sauce — see recipe page 92
finely chopped parsley

Soak the brains in a bowl of cold water, changing water twice. Discard skin from the brains and wash in tepid water, drain and place in a pan. Combine water, salt, onion stuck with cloves, vinegar, pep-

percorns and a bouquet garni of thyme, bay leaf and parsley in a pan and bring to the boil, cover and cook over low heat for 8−10 minutes. Strain liquid over the brains and bring back to simmering point, cover and simmer gently for 15 minutes, then strain well. Serve brains with béchamel sauce spooned on top and sprinkled with chopped parsley.

Casserole of Meat Balls and Vegetables

Serves: 4−6
Cooking time: 1½−1¾ hours

1 lb (500 g) lean lamb, ground
1 teaspoon thyme
1 teaspoon coriander
¼ teaspoon cayenne pepper
salt and pepper
1 egg
3 tablespoons oil
⅔ cup (165 ml) Beef Stock — see recipe
  page 90
⅓ cup white wine
2 medium onions, chopped
2 medium carrots, sliced
3 medium tomatoes, thickly sliced
4 medium potatoes, thickly sliced
10−12 green olives, pitted
10−12 black olives
1 lemon, sliced in rings
finely chopped parsley

Combine ground lamb in a bowl with thyme, coriander, cayenne pepper, salt, pepper and egg, mix well and form into small balls. Heat oil in a flameproof casserole, add meat balls and cook over moderately high heat, shaking casserole to brown the balls on all sides. Stir in stock and wine, cover and simmer over low heat for 45−50 minutes. Add onions, carrots, tomatoes, potatoes, green and black olives and lemon slices, cover and simmer a further 35−40 minutes, then serve, sprinkled with chopped parsley.
(Illustrated on page 27.)

Ragout of Lamb, Prunes and Oranges

Serves: 4–6
Cooking time: 2 hours

½ lb (250 g) pitted prunes
boiling water
4 tablespoons oil
2 medium onions, chopped
2 cloves garlic, crushed
1½ lbs (750 g) lamb, cubed
salt and pepper
1 teaspoon coriander
½ teaspoon thyme
¼ teaspoon ground bay leaves
1 cup (250 ml) Beef Stock — see recipe page 90
2 large carrots, cut into fingers
2 large potatoes, cut into pieces
4 medium tomatoes, thickly sliced
10–12 pitted green olives
1 medium orange, cut into rings
finely chopped parsley

Soak prunes in a bowl of boiling water for 15 minutes to plump. Heat oil in a flameproof casserole, add onions and garlic and sauté until onions are soft, add lamb cubes and cook until brown on all sides. Sprinkle with salt, pepper, coriander, thyme and ground bay leaves, cover and cook over moderately low heat for 10–12 minutes, pour in stock, cover and simmer gently for 1 hour. Add carrots and potatoes and simmer 20 minutes, add tomatoes, olives, orange slices and prunes, cover and simmer a further 15–20 minutes, then serve, sprinkled with chopped parsley.

Ragout of Lamb, Semolina and Chick Peas

Serves: 4–6
Cooking time: 2¾ hours

¼ lb (125 g) chick peas
water
salt and pepper
½ teaspoon thyme
1 bay leaf
3 tablespoons olive oil
1½ lbs (750 g) lamb shoulder, cut in pieces
2 medium onions, chopped
2 cloves garlic, crushed
1 cup (250 ml) dry white wine
1 cup (250 ml) Basic Bouillon — see recipe
  page 87
pinch of saffron
a bouquet garni
½ cup semolina
boiled rice

Soak the peas in a bowl of tepid water overnight, drain and place in a pan with water to cover, add salt, pepper, thyme and bay leaf and simmer over low heat for 1½ hours, drain and discard bay leaf. Heat oil in a flameproof casserole, add meat and cook over moderate heat until brown on all sides. Add onions and garlic and cook 3–4 minutes, add wine, bouillon, saffron, salt, pepper and a bouquet garni of thyme, bay leaf and parsley. Cover and simmer over low heat for 45 minutes, add chick peas and semolina and cook a further 20–25 minutes. Discard bouquet garni and serve with hot boiled rice.

Spicy Lamb Shanks

Serves: 4
Cooking time: 25–30 minutes

4 lamb shanks, trimmed

Marinade:
1 teaspoon dry mustard
½ teaspoon ground ginger
pinch of mace
3 teaspoons brown sugar, firmly packed
1 tablespoon lemon juice
3 tablespoons soy sauce
½ cup (125 ml) pineapple juice
6 tablespoons olive or salad oil

For the marinade, combine mustard, ginger, mace, brown sugar and lemon juice in a bowl, and mix until smooth, stir in soy sauce, pineapple juice and oil and blend.
Place lamb shanks in a glass or enamel dish, add marinade, baste and set aside for 2 hours to marinate, basting occasionally, then drain meat well. Pour marinade into a pan and heat until simmering. Cook shanks on a grid over hot coals, or under the broiler, 4″ (10 cm) from heat for 25–30 minutes, turning often and basting with the hot marinade, then serve.

Brain Fritters with Parsley

Serves: 4
Cooking time: 25–30 minutes

4 sets of lamb's brains
cold water
tepid water
1 tablespoon malt vinegar
Wine Court-bouillon — see recipe page 87
oil for cooking
Fritter Batter — see recipe page 86
sprigs of fresh parsley
lemon slices

Soak the brains in a bowl of cold water to cover for 2 hours, changing water twice, and drain, carefully remove skin, rinse and soak in a bowl of tepid water with vinegar for 15 minutes and drain well. Place brains in a deep pan, add court-bouillon and bring to simmering point and simmer for 15 minutes, drain and cut in half.
Heat oil in a deep pan until hot, dip brains in batter, one at a time, add to the hot oil and cook until golden. Lift out with a slotted spoon, drain on paper towels and keep warm. Rinse the parsley and dry well, then carefully add to the hot oil (it will spit) and cook for a moment, then drain on paper towels and serve with brains and lemon slices.
(Illustrated on opposite page.)

Penny's Lamb in Pastry

Makes about 40
Cooking time: 40–50 minutes
Oven: 200°C 400°F

4 tablespoons oil
1 medium onion, finely chopped
1 clove garlic, crushed
2 medium tomatoes, peeled and chopped
1 teaspoon oregano
salt and pepper
1 cup chopped spinach
3 cups ground, cold roast lamb
¼ lb (125 g) feta cheese
1 packet puff pastry
¾ cup (185 g) melted butter

Heat oil in a large pan, add onion and sauté 4–5 minutes or until golden, add garlic and cook 1 minute. Add tomatoes, oregano, salt, pepper and spinach, cover and cook over moderately low heat for 8–10 minutes. Add ground lamb and feta cheese and cook 4–5 minutes or until heated through.
Cut puff pastry sheets into quarters, butter each quarter of a sheet, add 2 teaspoons of lamb mixture diagonally across the pastry and roll, tucking in ends to make neat little finger size rolls. Place rolls on a greased baking tray, cook in a hot oven for 20–25 minutes until golden and serve.

BRAIN FRITTERS WITH PARSLEY (RECIPE THIS PAGE) ▶

Lamb's Tongues in Caper Sauce

Serves: 4
Cooking time: 1½–1¾ hours

4 lamb's tongues
water
1 small onion stuck with 3 cloves
1 small carrot, diced
a bouquet garni
1 cup (250 ml) water
¾ cup (185 ml) dry white wine
3 tablespoons oil
1 tablespoon lemon juice
2 tablespoons chopped capers
finely chopped parsley

Trim, wash and scrub the tongues, then soak in water for 15 minutes, drain and place in a flameproof casserole with onion stuck with cloves, carrot, bouquet garni of thyme, bay leaf and basil, water and wine and bring to the boil, reduce heat, cover and simmer over low heat for 1¼–1½ hours or until tender.
Lift out tongues, skin, trim and carve into thin slices and keep warm. Combine oil and lemon juice to blend, pour into a pan and heat, add capers and simmer, stirring, for 4–5 minutes for a sauce. Serve tongue slices with sauce poured on top and sprinkled with chopped parsley.

Brains in Vinaigrette

Serves: 4
Cooking time: 15–18 minutes

4 sets lamb's brains
cold water
tepid water
1 tablespoon malt vinegar
Wine Court-bouillon — see recipe page 87
Herb Vinaigrette — see recipe page 92

Place brains in a bowl of cold water to cover and set aside to soak for 2 hours, changing the water twice, drain and carefully remove the skin. Rinse well and soak in a bowl of tepid water to cover, with vinegar added, for 15 minutes and drain. Place brains in a pan with court-bouillon and bring to the boil, reduce heat, cover and simmer gently for 15 minutes, drain and serve hot with vinaigrette.

Spicy Lamb Chops

Serves: 4
Cooking time: 1¼ hours
Oven: 160°C 325°F

8 lean neck lamb chops
flour
salt and pepper
2 tablespoons oil
2 medium onions, sliced
1 tablespoon butter
3 tablespoons tomato catsup
2 teaspoons Worcestershire sauce
juice of 1 lemon
dash of seasoned pepper
½ cup (125 ml) Vegetable Stock — see recipe
    page 90
½ cup (125 ml) white wine
finely chopped parsley

Toss chops in flour, seasoned with salt and pepper. Heat oil in a pan, add onions and sauté until transparent, then remove to a shallow ovenproof casserole. To pan juices, add butter and heat, add chops and lightly brown on each side, then remove to the casserole. Stir tomato and Worcestershire sauces, lemon juice and seasoned pepper into the pan and heat, stir in stock and wine, bring to the boil, then pour mixture over the chops. Cover and cook in a moderately slow oven for 50–55 minutes until meat is tender, then serve sprinkled with parsley.

Sautéed Potatoes

Serves: 6
Cooking time: 20–25 minutes

2 lbs (1 kg) small new potatoes
3 tablespoons butter
1 tablespoon oil
½ teaspoon salt

Peel the potatoes and dry well in a cloth. Heat butter and oil in a large pan over moderate heat, add potatoes in one layer and cook for 5–6 minutes, shaking pan gently to roll the potatoes until sealed and golden on all sides. Sprinkle with salt and shake pan to roll the potatoes, reduce heat, cover and cook a further 12–15 minutes, shaking often to avoid potatoes sticking to the pan. Pour off pan juices, cook 1–2 minutes and serve hot. A good accompaniment for roast lamb or grilled chops.

Lamb Stuffed Eggplant

Serves: 4
Cooking time: 45–50 minutes
Oven: 190°C 375°F

2 medium eggplant, cut in half, lengthwise
salt
3 tablespoons butter
1 tablespoon oil
1 lb (500 g) lean lamb, ground
1 small onion, finely chopped
1 clove garlic, crushed
1 small green bell pepper, seeded and finely
    chopped
2 tablespoons finely chopped parsley
½ teaspoon salt
seasoned pepper
1¼ cups (300 ml) tomato purée

Sprinkle eggplant halves with salt, place cut side down in a colander and allow to drain for 1 hour, then pat dry, spoon out half the flesh and reserve. Melt butter and oil in a large pan, add eggplant and lightly brown the cut edges, lift out and set aside. To pan juices add lamb, onion, garlic, green pep-

per, parsley, salt and seasoned pepper and cook over moderate heat, stirring, for 6–8 minutes to lightly brown, add reserved eggplant flesh, stir and cook 2–3 minutes. Spoon mixture into eggplant cases, making a mound and place in an ovenproof casserole dish, add tomato purée and cook in a moderately hot oven for 30 minutes, then serve.

Brains, Mushrooms and Onions in Wine Sauce

Serves: 4
Cooking time: 20–25 minutes

⅓ cup Beef Stock — see recipe page 90
½ cup (125 ml) red wine
a bouquet garni
1 clove garlic, crushed
4 sets of lamb's brains, soaked, cooked and
    drained
Sautéed Mushrooms — see recipe page 82
Braised Onions — see recipe page 20
1 teaspoon tomato paste
1 tablespoon flour
1 tablespoon melted butter
salt and pepper
finely chopped parsley

Combine stock, wine, a bouquet garni of thyme, parsley and bay leaf, and garlic in a pan and bring to simmering point, add the prepared brains and simmer for 15 minutes, then put pan aside and allow brains to cool in the stock. Lift out brains and drain, cut into thick slices and place in a hot dish, add cooked mushrooms and onions and keep warm.
Stir tomato paste into the stock and cook over high heat to reduce by one-third, then remove from heat and discard bouquet garni. Make a roux with flour and melted butter, add to the pan and stir until blended. Return pan to the heat and cook, stirring for 1–2 minutes, pour over the brains, mushrooms and onions and serve, sprinkled with chopped parsley.

▲ ROAST BARON OF LAMB (RECIPE PAGE 38)

▲ RACK OF LAMB IN TARRAGON (RECIPE PAGE 39)

Stuffed Loin Chops on Rice

Serves: 6
Cooking time: 45−50 minutes
Oven: 180°C 350°F

6 very thick loin chops
salt and pepper
2 teaspoons finely chopped fresh mint
4 tablespoons butter
1 medium onion, minced
1 medium sweet potato, diced
1 cup soft breadcrumbs, firmly packed
1 egg
1 tablespoon finely chopped parsley
2 tablespoons white wine
3 tablespoons Chicken Stock — see recipe
  page 90
boiled rice
3 medium tomatoes, cut in wedges
sprigs of parsley

Slit each chop to make a pocket and sprinkle the cavities with salt, pepper and mint. Melt half the butter in a pan, add onion and sauté until transparent, add sweet potato, cover and cook over moderate heat for 8−10 minutes, shaking pan often, until soft. Remove pan from heat and mash the sweet potato, add breadcrumbs, egg, chopped parsley, wine and stock and mix well. Spoon into the pocket in each chop, fasten with skewers and brush with remaining butter, place in a baking pan and cook in a moderate oven for 30−35 minutes until tender. Serve chops over hot rice and garnish with tomato wedges and parsley sprigs.

Roast Baron of Lamb

Serves: 12–14
Cooking time: 2½–2¾ hours
Oven: 230°C reduced to 180°C
         450°F reduced to 350°F

8–9 lbs (4 kg) baron of lamb, without loins
salt and pepper
1 tablespoon chopped mint
6 spring onions, trimmed to bulbs
4 small carrots, sliced
2 small lemons, peeled and sliced
3 tablespoons butter, melted
1½ cups (375 ml) dry white wine
1 tablespoon lemon juice

Garnish:
Sautéed Potatoes — see recipe page 35
1 large lemon
2 tablespoons butter
3 teaspoons sugar
20–24 spring onions, trimmed

Order the baron of lamb, without loins, from your butcher and have him remove rump knuckle and leg bone from each leg, leaving the tail and shanks intact. Lay the double legs, skin side down on a board, open out and sprinkle with salt, pepper and mint. Place half the spring onions, sliced carrots and lemon slices in each cavity, close firmly and secure with skewers. Brush the meat with melted butter, place in a large baking pan and cook in a very hot oven for 15 minutes to seal and brown. Reduce heat to moderate and cook for 1¾ hours, pour off all but 3 tablespoons of fat from the pan, then pour wine and lemon juice over the meat and continue cooking for a further 30 minutes for rare, 45 minutes for well done, basting 2–3 times. Lift out the meat to a serving dish and allow to rest for 10 minutes to set the meat, but keep warm. Stir and scrape the pan to deglaze, then put pan juices through a fine sieve into a sauce dish and keep warm.
Meanwhile, for the garnish, prepare and cook potatoes, place in a heated dish and keep warm. Peel the rind, without pith from the lemon and cut into thin strips, melt half the butter in a pan, add sugar and cook, stirring for 3–4 minutes for a syrup. Add lemon rind and sauté for 3–4 minutes

until golden, lift out and drain on paper towels. Add remaining butter to the pan with spring onions, stir, cover and cook over low heat for 8–10 minutes, then lift out, place around the lamb and strew lemon rind on top. Discard any pith from the peeled lemon and cut into very thin slices, arrange slices over the meat and serve.
(Illustrated on page 36.)

Kumquat Stuffed Lamb

Serves: 6
Cooking time: 1½–1¾ hours
Oven: 230°C reduced to 180°C
         450°F reduced to 350°F

4 lbs (2 kg) boned leg of lamb
3 tablespoons butter
salt and pepper
¼ cup dry white wine

Kumquat Stuffing:
6–8 kumquats
boiling water
6–8 whole cloves
½ cup (125 ml) water
½ cup sugar
1 cup soft breadcrumbs

For the stuffing, wash the kumquats and place in a bowl, cover with boiling water and set aside for 5–6 minutes, then drain well and insert 1 clove in each kumquat. Combine water and sugar in a pan and bring to simmering point, stirring to dissolve sugar, and simmer for 4–5 minutes for a syrup. Add kumquats, cover and simmer 10–12 minutes, then pour into a bowl, add breadcrumbs and stir until most of the liquid is absorbed and cool.
Wipe the lamb and lay on a board, skin side down, add the stuffing, roll and fasten securely with skewers or string. Place lamb on a rack in a baking pan and brush with butter, cook in a very hot oven for 15 minutes to seal and brown. Reduce heat to moderate, sprinkle meat with salt and pepper and cook for 45 minutes. Pour wine over the lamb and cook a further 15–20 minutes or until tender. Lift out lamb to a carving dish and allow to rest in a

warm place for 10 minutes. Meanwhile, heat the pan juices, stirring and scraping to deglaze, thicken if necessary with a roux of flour and butter or gravy mix and simmer 2−3 minutes, then pour into a sauce dish and serve with the lamb.

sprinkle with salt and pepper and cook a further 15−20 minutes until tender. Remove meat to a warm dish and allow to rest for 10 minutes in a warm place. Pour most of the fat from the pan, add flour, salt and pepper and heat, stirring, until bubbly. Stir in wine and stock and bring to the boil, stirring constantly, simmer 2−3 minutes, then pour into a sauce dish and serve with the lamb.

Pork and Herb Stuffed Lamb

Serves: 4−6
Cooking time: 1−1¼ hours
Oven: 230°C reduced to 180°C
          450°F reduced to 350°F

2−3 lbs (1−1½ kg) boned shoulder of lamb
3 tablespoons melted butter
salt and pepper
1 tablespoon flour
¼ cup rosé wine
¾ cup (185 ml) Beef Stock — see recipe page 90

Pork and Herb Stuffing:
3 tablespoons butter
1 medium onion, finely chopped
¾ cup soft breadcrumbs
⅓ cup (85 ml) Beef Stock — see recipe page 90
½ lb (250 g) ground pork
1 clove garlic, crushed
½ teaspoon thyme
3 tablespoons finely chopped parsley
pinch of allspice
salt and pepper
1 egg

For the stuffing, melt butter in a pan, add onion and sauté until transparent, then place in a bowl. Soak breadcrumbs in the stock and add to the onions. Add ground pork, garlic, thyme, parsley, allspice, salt, pepper and egg and mix until well blended. Open out the lamb shoulder on a board, skin side down and spread with the stuffing, roll up and skewer to fasten, or tie with string. Brush with melted butter, place in a baking pan and cook in a very hot oven for 15 minutes, to seal and brown. Reduce heat to moderate and cook for 30 minutes,

Rack of Lamb in Tarragon

Serves: 3−4
Cooking time: 50−60 minutes
Oven: 180°C   350°F

loin square of 7 ribs
1 tablespoon melted butter
1 tablespoon finely chopped tarragon
1 tablespoon firmly packed brown sugar
½ cup (125 ml) cider vinegar
salt and pepper
¼ cup Beef Stock — see recipe page 90
extra chopped tarragon

Have your butcher prepare the loin square into a rack of lamb by trimming rib tops to the bone for 2″ (5 cm). Score the meat side of the rack in a criss cross pattern and brush with melted butter, place in a baking pan and cook in a moderately slow oven for 30 minutes. Mix tarragon, brown sugar, cider vinegar, salt and pepper in a bowl until blended, brush over the meat and cook a further 20−25 minutes. Remove rack to a hot dish and keep warm. Discard fat from the pan and stir in remaining tarragon sauce and heat, stirring and scraping to deglaze pan, stir in stock and bring to simmering point. Serve the lamb sprinkled with extra tarragon and the sauce.

(Illustrated on page 36.)

▲

Mixed Meat Stew

Serves: 6
Cooking time: 3 hours

4 tablespoons oil
1 lb (500 g) lean mutton, cubed
½ lb (250 g) lean pork, cubed
½ lb (250 g) lean beef, cubed
3 medium onions, cut in wedges
salt and seasoned pepper
2 bay leaves
a bouquet garni
water
boiled potatoes
finely chopped parsley

Heat oil in a flameproof casserole, add the three meats and cook over moderately high heat to brown on all sides. Reduce heat and add onions, salt, seasoned pepper, bay leaves, a bouquet garni of thyme, parsley and sweet basil and add water to barely cover. Bring to the boil, reduce heat, cover and simmer over low heat for 2¼ hours. Remove cover and simmer a further 30 minutes, discard bay leaves and bouquet garni and serve with boiled potatoes, sprinkled with parsley.

Ragout of Mutton and Cabbage

Serves: 4—6
Cooking time: 2 hours

3 tablespoons butter
1 tablespoon oil
1½ lbs (750 g) mutton neck chops
1 teaspoon saffron
⅔ cup (165 ml) white wine
⅔ cup (165 ml) water
salt and pepper
1 teaspoon thyme
¼ teaspoon ground bay leaves
½ teaspoon oregano
10—12 small new potatoes
6—8 large cabbage leaves
boiling water

Heat butter and oil in a flameproof casserole, add meat and cook over moderate heat to brown on all sides, sprinkle with saffron and stir well. Add wine and water and sprinkle with salt, pepper, thyme, ground bay leaves and oregano and stir, cover and simmer for 1¼ hours. Add potatoes and simmer for 20 minutes. Meanwhile, blanch the cabbage leaves in a bowl of boiling water for 4—5 minutes and drain well, add to casserole and cook a further 8—10 minutes.

▼

SAUSAGE STUFFED LAMB (RECIPE PAGE 42) ▶

Lamb Curry

Serves: 4
Cooking time: 1½–1¾ hours

1 tablespoon oil
1 tablespoon margarine
1½ lbs (750 g) lean lamb, cubed
½ teaspoon ground cloves
1 tablespoon curry powder
½ teaspoon nutmeg
½ teaspoon cinnamon
1 teaspoon ground ginger
1 bay leaf
2 large onions, chopped
2 large tomatoes, peeled and chopped
salt and pepper
½ cup (125 ml) white wine
boiled rice
Lavash — see recipe page 88

Heat oil and margarine in a flameproof casserole, add lamb and brown on all sides. Add cloves, curry powder, nutmeg, cinnamon, and ginger and cook for 2–3 minutes. Add bay leaf, onions, tomatoes, salt, pepper and wine. Cover tightly and simmer gently for 1¼–1½ hours. Discard bay leaf and serve over hot boiled rice with lavash and curry accompaniments. (See page 88.)

Lamb Chops with Ham and Parmesan

Serves: 4
Cooking time: 30–35 minutes
Oven: 180°C 350°F

4 lamb chops
salt and pepper
1 teaspoon curry powder
4 tablespoons butter
⅓ cup heavy cream
4 slices ham
3 tablespoons grated Parmesan cheese
2 carrots, cut into thin slices
salted water
2 teaspoons extra butter

Trim the chops and sprinkle with salt, pepper and curry powder. Melt butter in a pan, add chops and cook 6–8 minutes to brown on both sides, lift out meat and place in an ovenproof casserole dish. Stir 2 tablespoons cream into pan juices, then pour over the chops and place a slice of ham on top. Mix grated cheese with remaining cream, spoon over the ham and cook in a moderate oven for 20–25 minutes, until golden brown.
Meanwhile, cook carrots in a pan of salted water for 10–12 minutes and drain well, add extra butter, salt and pepper and keep warm. Serve chops with buttered carrots.

Sausage Stuffed Lamb

Serves: 4–6
Cooking time: 1¼–1½ hours
Oven: 230°C reduced to 180°C
       450°F reduced to 350°F

3 lbs (1½ kg) boned shoulder of lamb
salt and pepper
4 tablespoons melted butter
¼ cup white wine
¼ cup Beef Stock — see recipe page 90
4 large carrots, cut into pieces
2 × 9 oz (310 g) cans cannellini (butter) beans
1 tablespoon extra butter
1 tablespoon brown sugar

Stuffing:
½ lb (250 g) sausage meat, ground
1 tablespoon finely chopped parsley
1 teaspoon finely chopped chervil
2 teaspoons finely chopped rosemary
salt and pepper
2 tablespoons water

For the stuffing, combine all ingredients together in a bowl and mix well. Trim the lamb and lay open on a board, skin side down, spread stuffing thickly on the meat, then roll and fasten with skewers or tie with string. Place meat on a rack in a baking pan, brush with melted butter, and cook in a very hot oven for 15 minutes to seal and brown. Reduce heat to moderate and cook for 45 minutes, pour wine and stock over the lamb and cook a further

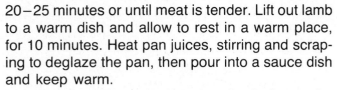

20–25 minutes or until meat is tender. Lift out lamb to a warm dish and allow to rest in a warm place, for 10 minutes. Heat pan juices, stirring and scraping to deglaze the pan, then pour into a sauce dish and keep warm.

Meanwhile, cook carrots in a pan of salted water for 10–12 minutes and drain, heat the beans and their liquid in a pan, simmer 2–3 minutes and drain. Combine carrots and beans in a warm serving dish, add extra butter and brown sugar and stir, cover and keep warm. Carve the lamb and serve with the vegetables and sauce.

(Illustrated on page 41.)

Prune and Apple Stuffed Hearts

Serves: 4
Cooking time: 1½–1¾ hours
Oven: 200°C   400°F

4 sheep's hearts, trimmed and soaked
salt and pepper
1¼–1½ cups (300–375 ml) Beef Stock — see
  recipe page 90
3 teaspoons flour
3 teaspoons butter
hot boiled rice
red currant jelly

Stuffing:
12 pitted prunes, soaked and finely chopped
1 large cooking apple, peeled and finely
  chopped
⅓ cup chopped walnuts
salt and pepper
1 tablespoon lemon juice
grated rind of ½ lemon
1½ cups soft breadcrumbs
1 egg
3 tablespoons melted butter
2 tablespoons water

For the stuffing, combine prunes, apples and walnuts in a bowl with salt, pepper, lemon juice and rind, breadcrumbs, egg, melted butter and water and mix well.

Spoon stuffing into the prepared hearts and close

with skewers, place in a greased baking pan and sprinkle with salt and pepper. Cover hearts with buttered waxed paper and add stock to the pan. Cook in a hot oven for 1½–1¾ hours, basting occasionally, and add more stock if liquid evaporates. Thicken pan juices with a roux of flour and butter and serve on a bed of hot rice with red currant jelly.

Honey Glazed Lamb

Serves: 4–6
Cooking time: 1–1¼ hours
Oven: 230°C reduced to 180°C
         450°F reduced to 350°F

4 lbs (2 kg) leg of lamb
⅓ cup warm honey
¼ teaspoon seasoned pepper
1 teaspoon cinnamon
1 teaspoon nutmeg
1 teaspoon ginger
water

Baste:
3 tablespoons warm honey
4 tablespoons lemon juice
½ teaspoon cinnamon
½ teaspoon nutmeg
½ teaspoon ginger

For the baste, combine all ingredients in a bowl, mix well and keep warm over a pan of simmering water.

Have your butcher bone the leg through the chump, leaving shank bone intact. Remove the skin and de-fat the lamb carefully, roll and fasten firmly with skewers or tie with string. Mix warm honey with seasoned pepper, cinnamon, nutmeg and ginger in a bowl and brush liberally over the leg to cover well. Place lamb on a rack over 1" (2½ cm) of water in a baking pan and cook in a very hot oven for 20 minutes to seal and brown the meat. Reduce heat to moderate, add water to pan to return to 1" (2½ cm) and brush meat liberally with the baste. Cook a further 50–55 minutes, basting well every 15 minutes. Lift out lamb to a warm carving dish and set aside to rest for 10 minutes in a warm place, then carve in thin slices and serve.

▲ LAMB CUTLETS IN PASTRY (RECIPE PAGE 46)

▲ CREAMED BRAINS AND MUSHROOMS (RECIPE PAGE 47)

44

Double Lamb Racks with Butter Beans

Serves: 4–6
Cooking time: 55–60 minutes
Oven: 180°C 350°F

2 loin squares, each of 6 ribs
4 tablespoons butter
½ cup (125 ml) dry white wine
salt and pepper
1 large onion, chopped
1 clove garlic, crushed
1 medium carrot, chopped
2 × 9 oz (310 g) cans cannellini (butter) beans
½ cup (125 ml) Chicken Stock — see recipe
   page 90
¼ cup cream

Have your butcher prepare the loins into racks of lamb by trimming rib tops to the bone for 2″ (5 cm) and sawing through the chine bone to separate into 2–3 portions for each rack. Cut the meat side in a diamond pattern and brush with 2 tablespoons melted butter, place in a baking pan and cover bone tips with foil. Cook in a moderate oven for 30 minutes, brush meat with half the wine, sprinkle with salt and pepper and cook a further 25–30 minutes.

Meanwhile, melt remaining butter in a pan, add onion and sauté until transparent, add garlic and carrot, cover and cook over low heat for 8–10 minutes, shaking pan occasionally. Add beans with the liquid, stock and remaining wine and bring to the boil, reduce heat, cover and simmer for 8–10 minutes. Stir in cream and heat, but do not boil, then serve with the lamb racks, cut into serving pieces.

Sweetbreads

Serves: 4
Cooking time: 18–20 minutes

1 lb (500 g) lamb sweetbreads
cold water
1 cup (250 ml) Wine Court-bouillon — see recipe
    page 87

To blanch and prepare sweetbreads, wash and soak them in a bowl of cold water for 3 hours, changing water 3–4 times until all trace of blood has been removed. Drain and place in a pan with court-bouillon, very slowly bring to the boil and boil for 8–10 minutes, lift out with a slotted spoon or strainer and plunge into cold water. Pat dry and carefully trim away gristle, connecting tissues and the membranes in the elongated throat, place in iced water to keep sweetbreads white and firm.

Sweetbread Fricassee

Serves: 4
Cooking time: 40–45 minutes

1 medium carrot, diced
1 stalk celery, finely chopped
1 large tomato, peeled and chopped
1 lb (500 g) Sweetbreads — see recipe above
3 slices bacon
2 cups (500 ml) Chicken Stock — see recipe
    page 90
salt and pepper
1 tablespoon butter
1 tablespoon flour
2 tablespoons heavy cream
finely chopped parsley

Place carrot, celery and tomato in a flameproof casserole, add prepared and drained sweetbreads and lay bacon slices on top. Add stock, salt and pepper, cover and simmer for 35 minutes. Lift out sweetbreads and keep warm, strain the stock into a bowl, reserving vegetables. Melt butter in a pan,

add flour and heat, stirring until bubbly, remove pan from heat and gradually stir in stock. Return pan to heat and bring to the boil, stirring until thick and smooth, then fold in cream and heat, but do not boil. Serve vegetables and sweetbreads, pour sauce on top and sprinkle with chopped parsley.

Lamb Cutlets in Pastry

Serves: 6
Cooking time: 30–35
Oven: 230°C reduced to 160°C
        450°F reduced to 325°F

6 lamb cutlets
Short Crust Pastry — see recipe page 86
1 egg, beaten with 2 teaspoons water
2 × 10 oz (310 g) cans cannellini (butter) beans
finely chopped parsley

Stuffing:
4 tablespoons butter
¼ lb (125 g) sausage meat, ground
½ teaspoon thyme
¼ teaspoon ground bay leaves
salt and pepper
¼ lb (125 g) mushrooms, minced
4 tablespoons heavy cream

For the stuffing, melt butter in a pan, add sausage meat and cook over moderate heat, stirring, until lightly browned. Spoon into a bowl, sprinkle with thyme, ground bay leaves, salt and pepper and mix well, add mushrooms and cream and mix until blended.

Trim the cutlets and lightly pound with a meat mallet. Divide pastry dough into 6 portions and roll out each portion into 8″ (20 cm) squares, cut off about 3″ (7½ cm) piece from one corner of each square and reserve for decoration. Cover each cutlet with stuffing, firming well and lay diagonally on pastry with rib bone protruding at cut off corner. Roll pastry over the cutlet, tucking in one end and firming at bone end, brush with egg glaze, decorate

with reserved off cut and glaze again with egg. Place on a greased baking tray and cook in a very hot oven for 8 minutes, reduce heat to moderately slow and cook a further 12–15 minutes.
Meanwhile, pour beans and liquid into a pan and heat through, drain well, sprinkle with chopped parsley and serve with the cutlets.
(Illustrated on page 44.)

Creamed Brains and Mushrooms

Serves: 4
Cooking time: 18–20 minutes

4 sets lamb's brains, soaked, cooked and
* drained*
6 tablespoons flour
salt and pepper
4 tablespoons butter
1 tablespoon oil
½ lb (250 g) button mushrooms
3 scallions, finely chopped
1 cup (250 ml) heavy cream
1 tablespoon Madeira or Marsala
1 tablespoon extra butter

Cut brains into quarters and dredge in 3 table-spoons flour seasoned with salt and pepper. Heat half the butter and half the oil in a large pan over moderate heat, add brains and cook until golden on all sides, lift out and keep warm.
Add remaining butter and oil to pan juices and heat, add mushrooms and sauté 3–4 minutes over low heat, add scallions and cook 2–3 minutes. Sprinkle with remaining flour and cook, stirring, for 1–2 minutes. Remove pan from heat, sprinkle with salt and pepper and stir in cream until blended, return pan to heat and cook over high heat to thicken and reduce liquid. Add brains and Madeira to the pan and cook, stirring, for 1 minute. Add extra butter in small pieces, stir until melted and blended, then serve immediately.
(Illustrated on page 44.)

Crumbed Sweetbreads

Serves: 4
Cooking time: 8–10 minutes

1 lb (500 g) Sweetbreads — see recipe on
* opposite page*
fine dry breadcrumbs
1 egg, beaten with 2 teaspoons water
3 tablespoons butter
1 tablespoon oil
Sautéed Mushrooms — see recipe page 82

Roll prepared and drained sweetbreads in bread-crumbs, shake off excess and dip in egg, then roll again in breadcrumbs. Heat butter and oil in a pan, add sweetbreads and cook over moderate heat until golden brown on all sides, lift out, drain on paper towels and serve hot with mushrooms.

Baked Potato Nests

Serves: 6–8
Cooking time: 25–30 minutes
Oven: 180°C   350°F

3 cups cooked, warm, mashed potato
2 whole eggs
2 egg yolks
6 tablespoons softened butter
⅓ cup thickened cream
½ teaspoon salt
small pinch of pepper
pinch of nutmeg
¼ cup extra butter, melted

Place warm mashed potatoes in a bowl, beat in whole eggs, egg yolks, softened butter and cream, beat briskly until light and fluffy, add salt, pepper and nutmeg and mix until blended. Spoon the mixture into a forcing bag with a round nozzle and flute nests or mounds onto a greased baking tray. Lightly rake the sides with a fork, spread melted butter on top, cook in a moderate oven for 25–30 minutes and serve.

▲

Irish Stew

Serves: 4
Cooking time: 2 hours

1½ lbs (750 g) lean neck chops
4 tablespoons flour
1 teaspoon salt
⅛ teaspoon seasoned pepper
3 tablespoons butter
1 tablespoon oil
3 medium onions, sliced
2 cups (500 ml) Beef Stock — see recipe
    page 90
4–5 medium potatoes, peeled and thickly sliced
1 teaspoon thyme
water
finely chopped parsley

Dredge the chops in flour mixed with salt and seasoned pepper, heat butter and oil in a flameproof casserole, add chops and lightly brown on all sides. Add onions, cover and cook over moderate heat 4–5 minutes, shaking casserole to avoid burning. Stir in stock and add potatoes, thyme, with water to barely cover, bring to simmering point and simmer gently for 1¾ hours. Thicken if necessary with leftover seasoned flour, simmer 2–3 minutes and serve sprinkled with chopped parsley.

Lamb Chops with Sautéed Potatoes

Serves: 4
Cooking time: 35–40 minutes

4 thick lean neck or forequarter chops
4 tablespoons oil
2 medium onions, chopped
3 medium tomatoes, peeled and chopped
1 clove garlic, crushed
salt and seasoned pepper
½ teaspoon thyme
½ teaspoon oregano
Sautéed Potatoes — see recipe page 35

Trim the chops and firm with the heel of hand. Heat oil in a large pan, add chops and cook until brown on each side, lift out and set aside. Add onions to pan juices and sauté 4–5 minutes until soft. Add tomatoes, garlic, salt, seasoned pepper, thyme and oregano and cook over moderate heat, stirring, for 4–5 minutes. Return chops to the pan, cover and cook over low heat for 20–25 minutes, or until chops are tender, then serve with sautéed potatoes.

▼

LAMB POT-AU-FEU (RECIPE PAGE 50) ▶

Sautéed Vegetables

Serves: 6–8
Cooking time: 20–25 minutes

4 tablespoons butter
1 medium onion, chopped
1 clove garlic, crushed
1 medium carrot, chopped
4 cups cooked, shredded cabbage
2 cups cooked rice
salt and seasoned pepper
1 cup (250 ml) Beef Stock — see recipe page 90
½ cup (125 ml) white wine or water

Melt butter in a large shallow pan, add onion and sauté until transparent, add garlic and carrot, cover and cook over low heat for 6–8 minutes, shaking pan occasionally. Stir in cabbage and rice, cover and cook over low heat to warm through. Stir in stock and wine or water and heat, stirring until hot, then serve.

Lamb Pot-au-Feu

Serves: 6
Cooking time: 3¼–3½ hours

4 tablespoons lard
3 lbs (1½ kg) breast of lamb or mutton
1 tablespoon sugar
1 clove garlic, crushed
1 small carrot, chopped
1 leek, chopped
1 small onion, chopped
½ stalk celery with leaves, chopped
a bouquet garni
salt and pepper
water
3 tablespoons oil
3 medium carrots, sliced
3 leeks, sliced
1 stalk celery, thickly sliced
3 medium onions, cut in wedges

Heat lard in a flameproof casserole until hot, add meat and cook until browned on all sides, sprinkle with sugar and add garlic, chopped carrot, leek, onion and celery with a bouquet garni of thyme, bay leaf and parsley. Sprinkle with salt and pepper and add water to cover. Bring to the boil and reduce heat, cover and simmer over low heat for 2½ hours, skimming fat from the surface occasionally. Lift out meat and discard bones, put stock and vegetables through a blender or fine sieve and return to a clean pan, return meat and bring back to simmering point. Heat oil in a pan, add sliced carrots, leeks, celery and onions and sauté over moderate heat for 4–5 minutes, then add to the casserole and continue simmering for 25–30 minutes. Lift out meat to a warm dish, with a slotted spoon lift out vegetables and arrange around the meat and keep warm. Strain the full flavor stock and serve as soup, followed by carved meat and vegetables.
(Illustrated on page 49.)

Apricot Rice Stuffed Lamb

Serves: 6
Cooking time: 1¼–1½ hours
Oven: 230°C reduced to 180°C
       450°F reduced to 350°F

4 lbs (2 kg) boned leg of lamb
4 tablespoons melted butter
salt and pepper
½ cup (125 ml) Beef Stock — see recipe page 90
2 tablespoons Marsala or Madeira

Apricot Rice Stuffing:
½ cup minced, dried apricots
1 cup cooked rice
3 tablespoons melted butter
1 tablespoon finely chopped parsley
2 teaspoons finely chopped chervil
¼ cup finely chopped celery leaves
small pinch of thyme
salt and pepper
¼ cup Marsala or Madeira

For the stuffing, combine all ingredients in a bowl and mix well. Wipe the lamb and pack the stuffing into the cavity, close and fasten securely with skewers or tie with string. Place meat in a baking pan and brush with butter, cook in a very hot oven for 15 minutes to seal and brown. Reduce heat to moderate, sprinkle with salt and pepper and cook for 40 minutes. Pour stock and Marsala over the meat and cook a further 20−25 minutes or until tender. Lift out lamb to a warm dish and allow to rest for 10 minutes in a warm place. Heat the pan juices, stirring and scraping to deglaze the pan, thicken with gravy mix and simmer 2−3 minutes, then pour into a sauce dish and keep warm. Carve the lamb and serve with the sauce.

together and rub into the cuts. Sprinkle the underside with salt and pepper, trim the flaps and fold over, then secure the meat firmly with string every 1″ (2½ cm) or so.

Place meat in a baking pan, add onion stuck with cloves, carrot slices and a bouquet garni of thyme, bay leaf and parsley. Pour stock over the meat and cook in a very hot oven for 15 minutes to seal the meat, then reduce heat to moderately hot. Combine breadcrumbs, salt, curry powder and pepper, spread thickly over the meat and cook for 35 minutes, basting 2−3 times with pan juices. Pour brandy over the meat and cook a further 12−15 minutes, lift out meat to a warm carving dish and allow to rest in a warm place for 10 minutes. Discard bouquet garni and onion from the pan, add chopped parsley and heat, stirring and scraping to deglaze the pan. Mash the carrot, then push through a sieve into a sauce dish and serve with the meat.

Crumbed Saddle of Lamb

Serves: 6
Cooking time: 1−1¼ hours
Oven: 230°C reduced to 190°C
      450°F reduced to 375°F

4½−5 lbs (2¼−2½ kg) trimmed saddle of lamb
   or young mutton
2 cloves garlic, crushed
5 anchovies, minced
5 peppercorns, crushed
salt and pepper
1 small onion, stuck with 3 cloves
1 medium carrot, thickly sliced
a bouquet garni
⅓ cup (85 ml) Beef Stock — see recipe page 90
½ cup fine dry breadcrumbs
½ teaspoon salt
½ teaspoon curry powder
dash of seasoned pepper
2 tablespoons brandy
2 tablespoons finely chopped parsley

Have your butcher remove the skin from the meat and excess fat from the underside. Cut a diamond pattern in the ridge of fat on the top, almost to the flesh. Mix garlic, anchovies and peppercorns

Barbecued Chops and Tomatoes

Serves: 4
Cooking time: 12−15 minutes

6 tablespoons oil
1 tablespoon chopped fresh basil
8 loin chops
salt and pepper
4 medium tomatoes
grated Parmesan cheese

Combine oil and basil in a bowl and mix well, brush chops on both sides with the mixture and place in a shallow glass or enamel dish, sprinkle with salt and pepper and set aside for 30 minutes. Brush chops again, place on the grill over medium hot coals and cook for 12−15 minutes, or cook 4″−6″ (10−15 cm) from heat under the broiler, until tender, turning often and basting. Meanwhile, cut tomatoes in half, place cut side to heat on the barbecue grid or broiler tray and cook for 3 minutes, turn tomatoes and cook a further 3 minutes. Sprinkle tomatoes with cheese and cook to lightly brown, then serve with the chops.

Lamb and Tomato Stew

Serves: 4–6
Cooking time: 1½–1¾ hours

1½ lbs (750 g) rib chops
4 tablespoons flour
salt and pepper
3 tablespoons butter
1 tablespoon oil
2 medium onions, cut in wedges
1 clove garlic, crushed
3 large tomatoes, peeled and chopped
1 tablespoon tomato paste
1 cup (250 ml) Vegetable Stock — see recipe
   page 90
½ cup (125 ml) white wine
2 teaspoons finely chopped mint
a bouquet garni

Trim the chops and dredge in flour, seasoned with salt and pepper. Heat butter and oil in a flameproof casserole, add chops and cook over high heat to brown on each side, lift out and set aside. To pan juices add onions and sauté until soft, add garlic and tomatoes and cook, stirring and mashing, for 5–6 minutes. Stir in tomato paste and blend, stir in stock, wine and mint. Add a bouquet garni of bay leaf, thyme and parsley and bring to the boil, reduce heat and simmer for 3–4 minutes. Return chops to the casserole and baste well, cover and simmer for 1¼–1½ hours or until chops are tender, discard bouquet garni and serve.

Curried Lamb and Apples

Serves: 4
Cooking time: 1¾–2 hours

4 tablespoons lard
1½ lbs (750 g) lamb or mutton neck chops,
    trimmed
3 medium onions, chopped
3 tablespoons butter or margarine
2 cloves garlic, crushed
1 tablespoon flour
1 tablespoon curry powder
1 teaspoon curry paste
1 tablespoon shredded coconut
1 teaspoon ground ginger
1¼ cups (300 ml) Beef Stock — see recipe
    page 90
3 large cooking apples, peeled and
    chopped
hot boiled rice
parsley

Heat lard in a flameproof casserole, add meat and 1 chopped onion and cook over high heat to sear chops on each side and brown the onion. Reduce heat, cover and cook 8–10 minutes.
Meanwhile, melt butter or margarine in a pan, add remaining onions and garlic and sauté until golden, add flour, curry powder and paste, coconut and ginger and cook, stirring for 2–3 minutes. Gradually stir in stock and bring to the boil, stirring constantly, then pour into the casserole, half cover and simmer over low heat for 1 hour. Add apples and simmer a further 35–40 minutes. Serve immediately with hot rice and garnish with parsley. For the best flavor, leave curry for 24 hours, heat and serve with curry accompaniments (see page 88).

Armenian Lamb

Serves: 4
Cooking time: 1½–1¾ hours

3 tablespoons butter
1 tablespoon oil
1 medium onion, chopped
2 cloves garlic, crushed
1 small red pepper, seeded and sliced thinly
1½ lbs (750 g) lean leg of lamb, cubed
1 teaspoon sugar
salt and seasoned pepper
1 teaspoon oregano
1¼ cups (300 ml) Beef Stock — see recipe
   page 90
⅓ cup (85 ml) plain yogurt
hot boiled rice

Heat butter and oil in a flameproof casserole, add onion and sauté 2–3 minutes, add garlic and red pepper and cook until soft. Add lamb cubes and cook over moderately high heat, stirring until lighly browned. Sprinkle with sugar, salt, seasoned pepper and oregano and stir in stock, cover and simmer over low heat for 1¼ hours or until tender. Stir in yogurt, heat and serve with boiled rice.

Crumbed Liver

Serves: 4
Cooking time: 10–12 minutes

1 large lamb's liver
salt and pepper
¼ cup lemon juice
4 tablespoons flour
1 egg
3 teaspoons water
½ cup dry breadcrumbs
4 tablespoons finely chopped parsley
6 tablespoons butter

Trim the liver, cut into ¼" (5 mm) slices, and place in a shallow dish, sprinkle with salt, pepper and lemon juice, set aside to marinate for 1 hour, then drain.
Mix flour with salt and pepper, beat egg with water and mix breadcrumbs with half the chopped parsley. Dredge liver slices in seasoned flour and shake off excess, dip in egg and coat with breadcrumb mixture, pressing in well.
Melt 4 tablespoons butter in a pan until hot, add crumbed liver slices and cook until golden brown, turning once or twice. Lift out and drain on paper towels and keep warm. Add remaining butter with remaining parsley to the pan juices and cook, stirring, for 1–2 minutes. Serve the liver and pour parsley butter sauce on top.

Teriyaki Lamb Kebabs

Serves: 4
Cooking time: 18–20 minutes

1½ lbs (750 g) lean lamb, cubed
2 medium onions, cut in wedges
1 small green pepper, seeded and cut in chunks
1 small red pepper, seeded and cut in chunks

Marinade:
⅓ cup dry sherry
⅓ cup pineapple juice
¼ cup soy sauce
1 tablespoon firmly packed brown sugar
2 cloves garlic, crushed
pinch of ground bay leaves
¾ teaspoon ground ginger

For the marinade, combine all ingredients in a blender and whirl until mixed and smooth. Place lamb cubes in a glass or enamel dish and add marinade, baste and set aside for 2 hours, then drain the marinade into a pan and heat to a simmer. Thread lamb on skewers, alternately with onion wedges and pepper chunks. Cook over hot coals or on a spit 4" (10 cm) from heat for 18–20 minutes or until tender, turning often and brushing with the heated marinade.

Crumbed Brains

Serves: 4–6
Cooking time: 10–12 minutes

4 sets lamb's brains, soaked, cooked and
    drained
1 tablespoon lemon juice
3 tablespoons oil
1 tablespoon finely chopped parsley
salt and pepper to taste
flour
1 egg, beaten with 2 teaspoons water
dry breadcrumbs
oil
chopped parsley
¼ cup dry white wine

Cut brains in half and place in a bowl, mix lemon juice, oil, parsley, salt and pepper in a jar, cover and shake briskly to blend, then pour over the brains and set aside to marinate for 30 minutes. Lift out brains and drain over the marinade, then toss in flour, dip in egg and roll in breadcrumbs. Heat oil in a pan until hot, add brains and cook until golden brown on all sides, lift out, drain on paper towels and keep warm. Pour marinade into a pan, add wine and heat, stirring, until simmering, for a sauce. Serve brains hot with the sauce.

Coffee Cream Lamb

Serves: 4–6
Cooking time: 1–1¼ hours
Oven: 230°C reduced to 180°C
       450°F reduced to 350°F

4 lbs (2 kg) boned leg of lamb
4 tablespoons flour
2 tablespoons instant coffee
3 tablespoons sugar
2 cups (500 ml) boiling water
⅔ cup (165 ml) heavy cream

Wipe the lamb, roll firmly and fasten with skewers or tie with string, rub flour in well and place in a baking pan. Cook in a very hot oven for 15 minutes

to seal and brown the meat, then reduce heat to moderate.
Meanwhile, dissolve coffee and sugar in a bowl with boiling water, cool and stir in cream until blended. Pour 1 cup of the coffee liquid over the lamb to cover and cook a further 50–60 minutes or until tender, basting every 15 minutes with about ½ cup of liquid. Lift out lamb to a dish and set aside in a warm place to rest for 10 minutes. Stir pan juices over heat to deglaze the pan, then pour into a sauce dish and keep warm. Carve lamb into thin slices and serve with the sauce.

Curried Lamb Chops

Serves: 4
Cooking time: 1½–1¾ hours
Oven: 180°C   350°F

3 tablespoons oil
1 tablespoon butter or margarine
1½ lbs (750 g) lean neck chops
1 large carrot, cut in thick slices
2 medium potatoes, thickly sliced
2 medium onions, cut in chunks
1 tablespoon flour
salt and seasoned pepper
3 teaspoons curry powder
1 tablespoon sweeet chutney
1 cup (250 ml) white wine
¼ cup Beef Stock — see recipe page 90
boiled rice
lemon wedges

Heat oil and butter or margarine in a pan, add lamb chops and cook over moderate heat until brown on both sides. Remove chops to an ovenproof casserole and add carrot and potatoes. To pan juices add onion chunks and sauté until golden, then remove with a slotted spoon to the casserole. Stir flour into the pan with salt, seasoned pepper and curry powder and cook, stirring, 3–4 minutes. Gradually stir in chutney, wine and stock and bring to the boil, stirring constantly, then pour over chops and vegetables. Cover and cook in a moderate oven for 1–1¼ hours. Serve with hot rice, garnished with lemon wedges and curry accompaniments. (See page 88.)

Cheese and Mint Stuffed Shoulder

Serves: 4–6
Cooking time: 1¼–1½ hours
Oven: 230°C reduced to 180°C
   450°F reduced to 350°F

3 lbs (1½ kg) boned shoulder of lamb
½ lb (250 g) riccota or fetta cheese
2 tablespoons finely chopped fresh mint
2 eggs
½ teaspoon freshly ground black pepper
6 tablespoons melted butter
salt and pepper
1 tablespoon flour
¼ cup white wine
½ cup (125 ml) Beef Stock — see recipe
 page 90
roasted potatoes, pumpkin and onions

Trim the lamb and lay on a board, skin side down. Mix cheese, mint, eggs and black pepper together in a bowl until blended, then spread over the meat for stuffing. Roll the meat over the stuffing firmly and fasten with skewers or tie with string. Place in a baking pan, brush liberally with melted butter on all sides and cook in a very hot oven for 15 minutes, to seal and brown. Sprinkle with salt and pepper, reduce heat to moderate and cook a further 1–1¼ hours. Lift out meat to a carving dish and allow to rest for 10 minutes in a warm place.

Meanwhile, discard most of the fat from pan, sprinkle with flour and stir over heat, add wine, stir and scrape to deglaze pan, add stock and bring to the boil, stirring constantly, then pour into a sauce dish. Carve meat and serve with the sauce and roasted vegetables.

LAMB WITH HERB MUSTARD (RECIPE PAGE 58) ▶

Marinated Lamb with Mushrooms and Tomatoes

Serves: 4
Cooking time: 18–20 minutes

1½ lbs (750 g) lean lamb
2 medium onions
2 medium tomatoes
¼ lb (125 g) mushrooms
¾ cup (185 ml) Herb Baste — see recipe
    page 91

Cut the lamb into cubes, onions and tomatoes into wedges and discard stems from the mushrooms. Place lamb cubes in a glass or enamel dish, add baste and stir to coat the meat, cover and chill for 2 hours. Lift out lamb cubes and thread on skewers, alternately with onion wedges, mushrooms and tomato wedges and cook 4″–6″ (10–15 cm) from heat in a pre-heated broiler for 18–20 minutes, turning often and basting with the baste, then serve.

Lamb with Herb Mustard

Serves: 6–8
Cooking time: 1½–1¾ hours
Oven: 230°C reduced to 180°C
          450°F reduced to 350°F

3 tablespoons French mustard
3 teaspoons soy sauce
1 clove garlic, crushed
1 teaspoon rosemary
¼ teaspoon ground ginger
1 tablespoon olive oil
4 lbs (2 kg) leg of lamb
¼ cup dry white wine
3 large potatoes
1 large sweet potato or yam
½ lb (250 g) pumpkin
salted water
oil for cooking

Combine mustard, soy sauce, garlic, rosemary and ginger in a blender for 1 minute, add olive oil, a drop at a time, through the hole in lid insert and blend until thick and smooth. Trim the lamb and wipe with a cloth, brush herb mustard liberally over the meat and place on a rack in a baking pan. Cook in a very hot oven for 15 minutes to seal and brown, reduce heat to moderate and cook a further 50–60 minutes, basting 2–3 times.

Meanwhile, peel and cube the potatoes, peel and thickly slice sweet potatoes and cut pumpkin into pieces, peel and seed. Place vegetables in a pan of salted water, bring to the boil and cook 2–3 minutes, then drain in a colander. Heat oil in a large pan until hot, add the vegetables and cook until golden brown, turning once or twice, lift out to a serving dish and keep warm.

Place meat on a carving dish and allow to rest for 10 minutes in a warm place, then carve. Strain the pan juices into a sauce dish and serve with the lamb and vegetables.

(Illustrated on page 57.)

Marinated Lamb Shanks

Serves: 4
Cooking time: 1¼–1½ hours
Oven: 180°C   350°F

4 lamb shanks
4 tablespoons flour
salt and pepper
3 tablespoons butter
3 tablespoons oil
⅓ cup light beer
hot cooked rice

Marinade:
1 clove garlic, crushed
2 tablespoons finely chopped celery leaves
½ teaspoon salt
dash of seasoned pepper
1 teaspoon finely chopped fresh mint
1¼ cups (300 ml) dry white wine
⅓ cup light beer

For the marinade, combine garlic, celery leaves, salt, seasoned pepper, mint and wine in a blender and whirl until mixed and smooth, then add beer. Place lamb shanks in a large dish in one layer, pour marinade over the meat and set aside for at least 2 hours. Lift out the shanks, but reserve marinade, and drain, roll in flour, seasoned with salt and pepper and shake off excess. Heat butter and oil in a large pan, add meat and brown on all sides, then remove to an ovenproof casserole dish. Add 1 tablespoon of leftover seasoned flour to the pan juices and heat, stirring, 1−2 minutes, stir in reserved marinade and heat, stirring and scraping to deglaze the pan, bring to the boil and pour over the shanks. Add beer, cover and cook in a moderate oven for 1−1¼ hours or until tender, turning once or twice, then serve over hot ice.

Heat butter and oil in a pan, add onion and green pepper and sauté over moderate heat for 4−5 minutes. Turn into a bowl and combine with ground lamb, parsley, celery, eggs, salt, seasoned pepper, cloves, breadcrumbs, nutmeg and stock and mix well. Pack into a greased loaf pan and cook in a moderate oven for 1¼ hours or until loaf leaves the pan sides, then unmold onto an oven tray. Increase heat of oven to hot. Meanwhile, in a bowl whip the mashed potatoes with extra butter, salt, pepper and nutmeg, add spinach and mix well. Spread mixture over the loaf to cover and cook in a hot oven for 10−12 minutes or until brown. Serve sliced with béchamel sauce.

Lamb Loaf

Serves: 4−6
Cooking time: 1¾ hours
Oven: 180°C increased to 200°C
350°F increased to 400°F

3 tablespoons butter
1 tablespoon oil
1 medium onion, minced
½ a small green bell pepper, seeded and
  minced
1½ lbs (750 g) lean lamb, ground
2 tablespoons minced parsley
½ stalk celery, minced
2 eggs
1 teaspoon salt
dash of seasoned pepper
⅛ teaspoon ground cloves
1 cup soft breadcrumbs
⅛ teaspoon nutmeg
½ cup (125 ml) Beef Stock — see recipe
  page 90
1½ cups hot mashed potatoes
1 teaspoon extra butter
salt and pepper
pinch of nutmeg
1 cup cooked spinach, minced
Béchamel Sauce — see recipe page 92

Lamb Risotto

Serves: 4−6
Cooking time: 1−1¼ hours

3 tablespoons butter
1 tablespoon oil
1 medium onion, finely chopped
1 clove garlic, crushed
1 lb (500 g) lean lamb, diced
salt and seasoned pepper
½ teaspoon oregano
2 medium tomatoes, chopped
⅓ cup Marsala or Madeira
1 bay leaf
½ cup (125 ml) water
1 cup long grain rice
1¾ cups (435 ml) Beef Stock — see recipe
  page 90
grated Parmesan cheese

Heat butter and oil in a flameproof casserole, add onion and sauté until soft, add garlic and cook 1 minute, add diced lamb and cook over moderate heat to brown on all sides, sprinkle with salt, seasoned pepper and oregano, add tomatoes, Marsala, bay leaf and water. Bring to the boil, reduce heat, cover and simmer for 35 minutes, add rice and stir in stock. Heat to a simmer and cook a further 18−20 minutes. Add grated cheese and stir, then serve with grated Parmesan cheese on top.

▲

Citrus Lamb Chops

Serves: 4
Cooking time: 1½ hours

1½ lbs (750 g) middle neck lamb chops
4 tablespoons flour
salt and pepper
4 tablespoons oil
⅓ cup lime or lemon juice
3 teaspoons finely chopped thyme
½ teaspoon cinnamon
½ teaspoon saffron
small pinch of cayenne pepper
seasoned pepper
½ cup (125 ml) sweet white wine
⅓ cup (85 ml) water

Trim the chops and toss in flour mixed with salt and pepper. Heat oil in a flameproof casserole, add chops and cook over high heat to quickly brown on each side. Reduce heat, sprinkle chops with lime juice then with thyme, cinnamon, saffron, cayenne pepper, salt and seasoned pepper and stir. Add wine and water, stir and baste the meat, cover and simmer over low heat for 1¼ hours and serve.

▼

Mutton and Tomato Stew

Serves: 4–6
Cooking time: 2 hours

3 tablespoons oil
2 large onions, chopped
1½ lbs (750 g) mutton, or lamb neck
chops
1 cup (250 ml) Beef Stock — see recipe page 90
½ cup (125 ml) water
a bouquet garni
4 large tomatoes, peeled and chopped
4 medium potatoes, quartered
salt and seasoned pepper

Heat oil in a flameproof casserole, add onions and sauté until transparent, add meat and cook over moderate heat until browned on all sides. Add stock, water and a bouquet garni of thyme, bay leaf and parsley, cover tightly and simmer for 1 hour. Add tomatoes, potatoes, salt and pepper to taste, cover and simmer a further 45 minutes, discard bouquet garni, then serve.

MARINATED LAMB IN PASTRY (RECIPE PAGE 62) ▶

Lamb Kidneys in Marsala

Serves: 4
Cooking time: 40–50 minutes

1 lb (500 g) lamb's kidneys
boiling water
juice of 1 lemon
4 tablespoons butter
salt and pepper
grated rind of ½ lemon
⅔ cup (165 ml) Marsala
finely chopped parsley

Skin, trim, halve and core the kidneys and place in a bowl, add boiling water to cover, lemon juice, and let stand for 2 minutes, then drain well and cut into small pieces. Melt butter in a pan until hot, add kidneys, sprinkle with salt, pepper and lemon rind and cover tightly. Cook over low heat for 30 minutes or until tender, add Marsala and stir, increase heat to moderate and cook until liquid is reduced by half. Sprinkle liberally with chopped parsley and serve immediately.

Marinated Lamb in Pastry

Serves: 4–6
Cooking time: 1–1¼ hours
Oven: 200°C increased to 230°C
            reduced to 200°C
            400°F increased to 450°F
            reduced to 400°F

4 lbs (2 kg) leg of lamb
Mint Marinade and Baste — see recipe page 91
4 tablespoons grated hard Cheddar cheese
salt and pepper
1 packet of frozen puff pastry, thawed
1 egg, beaten with 2 teaspoons water

Have your butcher bone the leg, leaving shank bone intact. Roll the meat neatly and fasten with skewers, lay in a large dish and pour marinade over the top, then set aside to marinate for 2 hours. Lift out the lamb, but reserve marinade, place in a baking pan, sprinkle with grated cheese, salt and pepper and cook in a hot oven for 30 minutes to seal and partly cook. Remove meat to a dish, but reserve pan juices, and allow to cool for 30 minutes, then remove skewers.
Roll out pastry ¼" (5 mm) thick, place meat on top and roll to cover, leaving shank bone end exposed. Brush with egg glaze, place on a ridged baking tray and cook in a very hot oven for 15 minutes, reduce oven to hot and cook a further 18–20 minutes. Lift out meat and slide on to a rack, place rack in a pan and allow meat to rest for 10 minutes in a warm place.
Meanwhile, stir reserved marinade into reserved pan juices and heat, stirring to deglaze and bring to the boil, then pour into a sauce dish and serve with the lamb.
(Illustrated on page 61.)

Bombay Lamb Curry

Serves: 6
Cooking time: 1–1¼ hours

2 lbs (1 kg) very lean lamb
3 tablespoons oil
1 large onion, finely chopped
1 clove garlic, crushed
1 teaspoon minced fresh ginger root
1 tablespoon (20 ml) curry paste
1 cup (250 ml) Vegetable Stock — see recipe
*   page 90*
1 cup (250 ml) sour cream
hot boiled rice
Lavash — see recipe page 88

Trim any fat from the lamb and dice the meat. Heat oil in a flameproof casserole, add onion, garlic and ginger and sauté 3–4 minutes over moderately low heat. Stir in curry paste and cook, stirring, for 2–3 minutes, stir in stock and add lamb, cover and simmer gently for 50–55 minutes or until meat is tender. Stir in sour cream and cook 4–5 minutes until simmering, then serve over hot rice with lavash and curry accompaniments. (See page 88.)

Garlic Kidneys with Lemon

Serves: 3–4
Cooking time: 12–15 minutes

8 lamb's kidneys
salt and pepper
3 tablespoons butter
1 tablespoon oil
2 cloves garlic, crushed
2 tablespoons lemon juice
hot boiled rice (optional)

Skin, core and quarter the kidneys and sprinkle with salt and pepper. Heat butter and oil in a pan, add garlic and sauté 2–3 minutes, add kidneys and cook over moderate heat, stirring, until brown on all sides. Add lemon juice and baste kidneys well, cover and simmer over low heat for 6–8 minutes. Serve over hot rice.

Brains in Bacon

Serves: 4
Cooking time: 30 minutes
Oven: 180°C 350°F

1 small onion, minced
¼ lb (125 g) mushrooms, finely chopped or minced
1 tablespoon finely chopped parsley
1 teaspoon finely chopped mint
1 teaspoon finely chopped chives
8 slices of bacon
4 sets lamb's brains, soaked and skinned
1 teaspoon prepared mild mustard
1 tablespoon softened butter
1 clove garlic, halved
salt and pepper
a bouquet garni
¾ cup (185 ml) dry white wine
¾ cup (185 ml) Chicken Stock — see recipe page 90
hot cooked rice

Combine minced onion and mushrooms in a bowl with parsley, mint and chives and mix well, then spread over the bacon slices. Add one brain to each bacon slice, wrap firmly and tie with string, then place in one layer in an ovenproof casserole dish. Mix mild mustard with softened butter until blended and add to the casserole with garlic halves, salt, pepper and a bouquet garni of thyme, bay leaf and parsley. Add wine and stock, cover and cook in a moderate oven for 30 minutes, discard bouquet garni and garlic and serve hot over a bed of hot cooked rice.

Curried Lamb Kebabs

Serves: 4
Cooking time: 45–50 minutes

1½ lbs (750 g) lean lamb
very thinly sliced ginger root
3 tablespoons oil
1 medium onion, finely chopped
3 cloves garlic, crushed
1 tablespoon curry powder or paste
½ teaspoon chilli powder
1 teaspoon cinnamon
¼ teaspoon ground cloves
1¼ cups (300 ml) Vegetable Stock — see recipe page 90
½ teaspoon mixed spices
hot boiled rice
Lavash — see recipe page 88

Cut lamb into cubes and thread on skewers with one slice of ginger between cubes. Heat oil in a large pan, add kebabs and cook over high heat, turning often, until meat is browned, then lift out and set aside. To pan juices and onion and garlic and sauté over moderately low heat for 3–4 minutes, stir in curry powder or paste, chilli powder, cinnamon and cloves and cook, stirring, for 2–3 minutes. Stir in stock, return kebabs to the pan and baste, cover and simmer over low heat for 30–35 minutes or until meat is tender, sprinkle with mixed spices and cook 1–2 minutes, basting, then serve over hot rice with lavash and curry accompaniments. (See page 88.)

Lamb's Tongues with Carrots and Peas

Serves: 6
Cooking time: 1½–1¾ hours

6 lamb's tongues
water
3 cups (375 ml) Wine Court-bouillon — see
   recipe page 87
2 medium carrots, sliced
½ lb (250 g) shelled green peas
boiling salted water
3 tablespoons butter
salt and pepper
1 teaspoon finely chopped fresh mint
3 slices bacon, cut into pieces
1 tablespoon brown sugar
chopped parsley

Trim, wash and scrub the tongues and soak in a bowl of water for 15 minutes, drain and place in a deep pan with court-bouillon, bring to simmering point and simmer over low heat for 1¼–1½ hours, then lift out, drain and skin.

Meanwhile, cook carrots and peas in separate pans of boiling salted water for 10–12 minutes and drain, add 2 teaspoons of butter with salt, pepper and mint to the peas, cover and keep warm, set carrots aside.

Cook bacon pieces in a large pan for 5–6 minutes and lift out, drain on paper towels and keep warm. Add remaining butter to pan juices, add tongues and cook until brown. Lift out and place with the bacon. Add brown sugar to pan juices and stir until dissolved, add cooked carrot slices and sauté 2–3 minutes. Serve carrots, topped with tongues, bacon and peas and sprinkled with parsley.

Garlic Lamb in Coffee

Serves: 4–6
Cooking time: 1¼ hours
Oven: 180°C 350°F

4 lbs (2 kg) leg of lamb, boned
8–10 cloves garlic, slivered
4 tablespoons flour
2 tablespoons instant coffee
2 cups (500 ml) boiling water
1 cup (250 ml) red wine
salt and pepper

Trim and wipe the lamb, roll firmly and skewer to fasten or tie with string, make many incisions over the leg and insert garlic slivers to flavor the meat with garlic. Sprinkle flour over the meat and rub in well, place in a baking pan and cook in a moderate oven for 30 minutes.

In a bowl dissolve coffee in boiling water and add wine, pour 1 cup over the lamb and cook a further 40–45 minutes, basting well every 10 minutes with ⅔ cup of coffee-wine liquid. Lift lamb to a warm dish and set aside for 10 minutes in a warm place to rest and set the meat. Add salt and pepper to pan juices, bring to simmering and pour into a sauce dish. Serve lamb thinly sliced with the sauce.

Grilled Sweetbreads and Tomatoes

Serves: 4
Cooking time: 10–12 minutes

1 lb (500 g) Sweetbreads — see recipe page 46
flour
salt and pepper
¼ cup salad oil
4 medium tomatoes, cut in half
½ cup (125 g) melted butter
1 teaspoon lemon juice
Sautéed Mushrooms — see recipe page 82

Roll drained sweetbreads in flour seasoned with salt and pepper and dip in oil, place on a rack with tomatoes, cut side down and broil 3″ (7½ cm) from heat for 5–6 minutes. Turn both sweetbreads and tomatoes, brush tomatoes with a little melted butter and broil a further 5–6 minutes. Mix melted butter and lemon juice together and serve with sweetbreads, tomatoes and mushrooms.

Casserole of Lamb with Anchovies

Serves: 4
Cooking time: 55–60 minutes
Oven: 230°C reduced to 180°C
       450°F reduced to 350°F

¼ cup olive oil
1½ lbs (750 g) lean lamb, cubed
1 teaspoon basil
½ teaspoon salt
dash of pepper
1 tablespoon flour
1 clove garlic, crushed
⅓ cup white wine
1 cup (250 ml) Chicken Stock — see recipe
   page 90
3 anchovies
finely chopped parsley

Heat oil in a large pan, add lamb cubes and cook until brown on all sides, spoon lamb into an oven-proof casserole dish and sprinkle with basil, salt, pepper and flour, add garlic and stir well. Cook in a pre-heated hot oven for 8–10 minutes, then reduce heat to moderate.

Meanwhile, add wine to the pan juices and bring to the boil, stirring and scraping to deglaze the pan, stir in stock and heat until boiling, then pour over the lamb. Cover the casserole and cook for 35–40 minutes or until lamb is tender. Finely chop or mince the anchovies and stir into the casserole, then serve, sprinkled with chopped parsley.

Navarin of Lamb

Serves: 4
Cooking time: 2¼ hours
Oven: 160°C   325°F

3 tablespoons lard
1½ lbs (750 g) boned lamb shoulder,
    cubed
3 tablespoons butter
1 tablespoon oil
2 medium onions, cut in wedges
2 cloves garlic, crushed
3 tablespoons flour
½ teaspoon sugar
1 teaspoon salt
seasoned pepper
¾ cup (185 ml) Beef Stock — see recipe
    page 90
¼ cup dry white wine
½ stalk celery, chopped
a bouquet garni
3 medium carrots, sliced
4 large potatoes, thickly sliced
finely chopped parsley

Melt lard in a large pan, add lamb and cook until brown on all sides, then remove to an ovenproof casserole. In a clean pan heat butter and oil, add onions and sauté until lightly browned, add garlic, flour, sugar, salt and seasoned pepper and cook, stirring, for 1–2 minutes. Stir in stock and wine and bring to the boil, then pour over the lamb. Add celery and a bouquet garni of thyme, bay leaf and parsley, cover and cook in a moderately slow oven for 1½ hours. Add carrots and potatoes and cook a further 30 minutes, discard bouquet garni and serve, sprinkled with parsley.

BRAISED LAMB SHANKS (RECIPE PAGE 68) ▶

Grilled Lamburgers

Serves: 4
Cooking time: 8—10 minutes

1½ lbs (750 g) lean lamb, ground
1 medium onion, minced
1 teaspoon salt
½ cup minced parsley
1 egg
3 tablespoons oil
4—6 slices bacon

Combine lamb, onion, salt, parsley and egg in a bowl and mix well, form into 4—6 thick patties and brush with oil. Wrap bacon slices around the patties and brush again with oil, place on the rack and broil for 8—10 minutes, turning often, then serve.

Braised Lamb Shanks

Serves: 4
Cooking time: 1½—1¾ hours
Oven: 180°C reduced to 160°C
      350°F reduced to 325°F

4 meaty lamb shanks
4 tablespoons bacon drippings
1 tablespoon sugar
1 cup (250 ml) boiling water
1½ cups (375 ml) Beef Stock — see recipe
  page 90
2 medium turnips, cubed
4 large carrots, cut in half
2 leeks, white part only, sliced
4 medium onions, peeled
2 cloves garlic, crushed
¼ lb (125 g) French beans, sliced
¼ of a small cabbage, leaves separated
1 teaspoon salt
⅛ teaspoon pepper
a bouquet garni
2 teaspoons arrowroot
½ cup (125 ml) red wine

Wash the shanks and discard thin parchment cover. Heat bacon drippings in a large pan, add shanks and cook over moderately high heat to lightly brown on all sides. Sprinkle with sugar and cook over high heat for 3—4 minutes to caramelize the sugar over the meat, then lift out shanks and place in an ovenproof casserole.
Add boiling water to the pan, stir and scrape to deglaze, stir in stock and heat, then add to the casserole. Add turnips, carrots, leeks, onions, garlic, beans, cabbage, salt, pepper and a bouquet garni of thyme, bay leaf and parsley. Cover and cook in a moderate oven for 30 minutes, reduce heat to moderately slow and cook for 30 minutes. Mix arrowroot with wine until smooth, stir into the casserole and cook a further 15—20 minutes or until meat is tender. Discard bouquet garni, adjust seasoning and serve.
(Illustrated on page 67.)

Devilled Lamb Kidneys

Serves: 4
Cooking time: 12—15 minutes

8 lamb's kidneys
cold water
6 tablespoons butter
½ teaspoon prepared hot mustard
2 teaspoons Worcestershire sauce
2—3 drops Tabasco sauce
1 teaspoon minced onion
1 teaspoon minced chives

Marinade:
4 tablespoons salad oil
salt and pepper
½ teaspoon finely chopped thyme
¼ teaspoon prepared hot mustard
⅛ teaspoon mace

For the marinade, mix all ingredients in a jar, cover and shake briskly until blended.
Trim the kidneys and soak in a bowl of cold water for 1 hour, drain and pat dry, cut into halves and discard the core, cut into quarters and place in a dish. Add marinade and baste, set aside for 30—40 minutes to marinate, then drain well.

Melt 3 tablespoons of butter in a pan, add kidneys and cook over moderately high heat to brown on all sides, reduce heat and cook over low heat for 7–8 minutes, stirring often, then lift out and keep warm. Meanwhile, melt remaining butter in a pan, add mustard, Worcestershire and Tabasco sauces, onion and chives and stir over moderately low heat until blended, then serve over the kidneys.

Marinated Lamb Curry

Serves: 4
Cooking time: 1¼–1½ hours

1½ lbs (750 g) lean leg lamb, cubed
½ cup (125 ml) plain yogurt
2 teaspoons mixed spices
¼ teaspoon cayenne pepper
½ cup raisins
½ cup chopped dried apricots
½ cup (125 ml) boiling water
3 tablespoons butter
1 tablespoon oil
2 medium onions, chopped
1 clove garlic, crushed
3 teaspoons curry powder
1 teaspoon salt
½ teaspoon chili sauce
1 tablespoon chutney
½ cup (125 ml) Vegetable Stock — see recipe
   page 90
1 tablespoon lemon juice
hot boiled rice

Place lamb cubes in a bowl, combine yogurt, mixed spices and cayenne pepper and mix, then pour over the lamb, baste and set aside for at least 2 hours to marinate, basting occasionally, then drain, reserving marinade. Combine raisins and apricots in a bowl, add boiling water and soak for 15 minutes to plump, then drain and set aside, reserving liquid.
Heat butter and oil in a flameproof passerole, add onions and sauté 2–3 minutes, add garlic and cook 1 minute. Sprinkle with curry powder and salt, stir in chili sauce and chutney and cook 2–3 minutes,

add drained meat and fruit and cook, stirring, for 4–5 minutes. Stir in reserved marinade, fruit liquid and stock and bring to the boil, reduce heat, cover and simmer over low heat for 1 hour, stir in lemon juice, heat and serve hot with hot rice.

Lamb and Rosemary in Lemon Sauce

Serves: 4
Cooking time: 1–1¼ hours
Oven: 230°C reduced to 180°C
       450°F reduced to 350°F

4 tablespoons lard or bacon fat
1½ lbs (750 g) lean lamb, cubed
4 tablespoons flour
salt and pepper
1 teaspoon rosemary
1 clove garlic, crushed
½ cup (125 ml) Marsala or Madeira
2 cups (500 ml) Beef Stock — see recipe
   page 90
2 egg yolks
1 tablespoon lemon juice
finely chopped parsley

Heat the lard or bacon fat in a large pan, add the lamb cubes and cook until lightly brown on all sides, lift out meat and place in an ovenproof casserole dish. Sprinkle with flour seasoned with salt, pepper and rosemary and stir well, cook in a hot oven for 8–10 minutes, then reduce heat to moderate.
Meanwhile, add garlic to pan juices and cook 1 minute, stir in Marsala and bring to the boil, stirring and scraping to deglaze the pan. Simmer for 5–6 minutes to reduce liquid by half, stir in stock and bring to the boil, then pour over the lamb. Cover and cook for 35–40 minutes or until lamb is tender. Lift out lamb with a slotted spoon, place in a deep, hot serving dish and keep warm. Strain the stock through a fine sieve into a pan. Beat the egg yolks in a bowl, add lemon juice and beat until mixed, gradually add 1 cup of hot stock, beating constantly, until blended, then stir back into the stock and bring to the boil, stirring continually. Pour sauce over the lamb and serve, sprinkled with chopped parsley.

▲ SADDLE OF LAMB WITH ROSEMARY (RECIPE PAGE 72)

▲ SHEEP TONGUES WITH VEGETABLES (RECIPE PAGE 72)

Blanquette of Lamb

Serves: 4
Cooking time: 2 hours

3 tablespoons oil
1½ lbs (750 g) lean neck chops
1 large onion, sliced
4–6 medium onions, peeled
4 small carrots, sliced
1 large potato, sliced
salt and pepper
½ teaspoon basil
2 teaspoons finely chopped mint
1½ cups (375 ml) Beef Stock — see recipe
    page 90
a bouquet garni
¼ lb (125 g) mushrooms, sliced
1 tablespoon butter
1 tablespoon flour
1 tablespoon lemon juice
½ cup (125 ml) white wine
1 egg
¼ cup cream
2 tablespoons minced parsley

Heat oil in a flameproof casserole, add lamb chops and sauté until browned on all sides, add sliced onion, whole onions, carrots and potato, cover and cook over moderately low heat for 8–10 minutes, shaking casserole occasionally. Sprinkle with salt, pepper, basil and mint and stir in stock, add a bouquet garni of thyme, bay leaf and parsley and bring to the boil. Reduce heat, cover and simmer over low heat for 1 hour. Add mushrooms and simmer a further 30 minutes, then discard bouquet garni. Melt butter in a pan, add flour and cook until bubbly, stir in lemon juice and wine and bring to the boil, stirring constantly until thick and smooth, then stir into the casserole and simmer 8–10 minutes. Beat egg and cream together and stir into the casserole. Heat, but do not boil, and serve hot, sprinkled with parsley.

Kidney and Bacon Kebabs

Serves: 4
Cooking time: 8–10 minutes

4 lamb's kidneys
4 slices bacon
8 small onions, peeled
Spicy Honey Baste — see recipe page 91
hot boiled rice

Skin, core and halve the kidneys, discard rind from bacon, cut slices in half and roll up. Par-boil onions for 2–3 minutes and drain. Thread kidney, bacon and onions, alternately, on skewers and brush well with the baste. Place kebabs on a grill 4"–6" (10–15 cm) from heat over medium hot coals or under the broiler and cook for 8–10 minutes, turning frequently and brushing with the baste, then serve on a bed of hot rice.

Saddle of Lamb with Rosemary

Serves: 4–6
Cooking time: 50–60 minutes
Oven: 230°C reduced to 200°C
      450°F reduced to 400°F

3½ lbs (1¾ kg) trimmed saddle of lamb
salt and pepper
2–3 sprigs of rosemary
4 tablespoons melted butter
1 medium carrot, sliced
1 medium onion, sliced
3 cloves garlic, halved
⅓ cup dry white wine
½ cup (125 ml) Beef Stock — see recipe
   page 90
½ teaspoon finely chopped rosemary

Have your butcher remove the skin and trim off fat leaving a ¼" (5 mm) layer on the meat, and discard excess fat from the underside. Make diamond cuts

over the meat only to the flesh, sprinkle underside with salt and pepper and lay rosemary sprigs along the meat. Close the flaps and secure the lamb firmly with string every 1" (2½ cm) or so.

Place meat in a baking pan and brush the ends with melted butter. Cook in a very hot oven for 15 minutes to seal and lightly brown, reduce oven to hot, add carrot, onion slices and garlic around the meat, and brush meat ends and vegetables with melted butter and pan juices. Cook a further 30 minutes for rare, 45 minutes for well done, basting meat ends 2–3 times. Lift out meat to a warm dish and allow to rest for 10 minutes in a warm place. Pour off all but 1 tablespoon of fat from the pan, add wine and stock and heat to simmering, stirring and scraping to deglaze the pan. Mash the vegetables. Add chopped rosemary with salt and pepper to taste and simmer 2–3 minutes. Push gravy through a sieve into a sauce dish and serve with the lamb, carved into thick chop slices. Sautéed mushrooms, sprinkled with rosemary, go well with this dish.
(Illustrated on page 70.)

Sheep Tongues with Vegetables

Serves: 6
Cooking time: 1½–1¾ hours

6 lamb's tongues
water
4 tablespoons olive oil
1 medium turnip, peeled and chopped
1 stalk celery with leaves, chopped
2 cloves garlic, crushed
3 large tomatoes, peeled and chopped
bunch of 16–18 spring onions, trimmed
3 large carrots, quartered
salt and pepper
a bouquet garni
½ cup (125 ml) Beef Stock — see recipe
   page 90
¼ cup red wine

Scrub and wash the tongues and soak in a bowl of water for 15 minutes, then drain. Heat oil in a flameproof casserole, add turnip, celery, garlic, tomatoes and half the spring onions, chopped. Cover and braise over moderately low heat for 8–10 minutes, stirring 2–3 times to juice the tomatoes. Add tongues, carrots, salt, pepper and a bouquet garni of thyme, bay leaf and parsley, cover tightly and simmer over low heat for 45 minutes. Add remaining whole spring onions, cover and simmer a further 35–40 minutes. Lift out carrots, whole spring onions and tongues, trim the tongues and slice each to the cartilage at the base. Discard bouquet garni and put the vegetable mixture through a blender to purée and return to a clean pan. Stir in stock and wine and heat, return tongues, carrots and spring onions to the pan, cover and cook 3–4 minutes or until heated through, then serve.

(Illustrated on page 70.)

Kebabs of Lamb and Apples

Serves: 4
Cooking time: 20–25 minutes

1½ lbs (750 g) lean lamb, cubed
3 cooking apples
2 tablespoons lemon juice
3 medium onions, cut in thick wedges
4–6 sprigs of rosemary

Marinade:
1 teaspoon ground ginger
3 teaspoons curry powder
salt and seasoned pepper
3 teaspoons soy sauce
3 tablespoons honey
⅓ cup (85 ml) dry white wine

For the marinade, combine all ingredients in a pan, stir and heat until boiling, remove pan from heat and cool.
Place lamb cubes in a dish, add marinade, baste and set aside for at least 1 hour, basting occasionally. Peel and core the apples and cut into thick wedges, place in a dish, add lemon juice and set aside for 6–8 minutes, basting once or twice. Drain lamb, but reserve marinade, and drain apples, pour juice into the marinade and stir.
Thread lamb cubes, onions, apples and rosemary alternately on skewers and baste with the marinade. Cook either on a grill over hot coals, or 4″–6″ (10–15 cm) from heat under the broiler, for 15–20 minutes, until browned and tender, turning often and basting with the marinade.

Hot Lamb Curry

Serves: 6
Cooking time: 1–1¼ hours

1 tablespoon oil
1 medium onion, finely chopped
4 cloves garlic, crushed
2 teaspoons minced fresh ginger root
1 medium green bell pepper, seeded and finely
   chopped
1 teaspoon turmeric
1 teaspoon mixed spices
½ teaspoon chili powder
2 lbs (1 kg) lean lamb, diced
3 medium tomatoes, peeled and finely chopped
1 tablespoon finely chopped mint
2 teaspoons salt
hot water
hot boiled rice

Heat oil in a flameproof casserole, and onion, garlic, ginger and green pepper and sauté over low heat until soft. Add turmeric, mixed spices and chili powder and cook, stirring 3–4 minutes, add diced lamb and cook, stirring, for 6–8 minutes to lightly brown. Cover and cook over very low heat for 20–25 minutes for lamb to absorb the flavors. Add tomatoes, mint and salt and stir, add hot water to barely cover and simmer, uncovered, for 30–35 minutes, then serve with hot rice and curry accompaniments. (See page 88.)

▲ STUFFED LEG IN PASTRY (RECIPE PAGE 76)

▲ MUTTON AND CABBAGE PIE (RECIPE PAGE 76)

Lamb and Endive Casserole

Serves: 4–6
Cooking time: 1½ hours
Oven: 160°C 325°F

3 tablespoons butter
1 tablespoon oil
6 lamb neck chops
1 large onion, chopped
1 clove garlic, crushed
2 lbs (1 kg) Belgian endive, trimmed
boiling water
2 whole cloves
1 teaspoon thyme
2 bay leaves
1 tablespoon chopped parsley
salt and pepper
1 cup (250 ml) Beef Stock — see recipe
   page 90

Heat butter and oil in an ovenproof casserole, add chops and cook over moderate heat until brown on all sides, add onion and garlic, cover and simmer over low heat for 15 minutes.

Meanwhile, blanch the endive in boiling water for 3–4 minutes and drain well. Add to the casserole with cloves, thyme, bay leaves, parsley, salt, pepper and stock. Cover and cook in a moderately slow oven for 1 hour. Carefully drain liquid into a pan and cook over high heat to reduce by ⅓ for a sauce. Serve chops and endive and pour sauce on top.

Stuffed Leg in Pastry

Serves: 6–8
Cooking time: 1½–1¾ hours
Oven: 200°C increased to 230°C reduced to
200°C
400°F increased to 450°F reduced to
400°F

6–7 lbs (3 kg) leg of lamb
4 tablespoons oil
Short Crust Pastry — see recipe page 86
1 egg, beaten with 2 teaspoons water
¼ cup (65 ml) Beef Stock — see recipe page 90

Stuffing:
3 tablespoons butter
1 tablespoon oil
¼ lb (125 g) mushrooms, minced
3 lamb kidneys, trimmed and minced
3 scallions, white only, minced
salt and pepper
small pinch of thyme
good pinch of rosemary
1½ cups soft breadcrumbs
¼ cup water
¼ cup Marsala, sherry or Madeira

For the stuffing, heat butter and oil in a pan, add mushrooms, kidneys and scallions and cook over moderate heat, stirring, for 5–6 minutes. Remove pan from heat and sprinkle with salt, pepper, thyme and rosemary, add breadcrumbs, stir in water and Marsala and mix well.

Have your butcher remove the leg bone through the chump end of the meat, leaving the shank bone intact. Wipe the meat and place on a board, pack stuffing into the cavity, bring sides together and skewer and loop with string to close securely. Place meat on a rack in a baking pan, brush with oil on all sides and cook in a hot oven for 30 minutes to seal, brown and partly cook. Lift out meat to a dish and set aside for 30 minutes, but reserve pan juices.

Place meat on a ridged baking tray and carefully remove skewers and string. Roll out pastry ¼" (5 mm) thick to a pear shape and place over the meat to cover, trim pastry, leaving ½" (1 cm) excess around the base, then tuck excess in under the leg. Cut leftover pastry into ½" (1 cm) strips to make a border around the base, a large ring around the top and pieces for decoration. Brush egg glaze over the pastry, place strips and pieces of pastry in position and brush with egg glaze.

Cook in a very hot oven for 15 minutes, reduce oven to hot and cook a further 20–25 minutes or until golden brown. Lift out tray and slide lamb onto a rack, place in a pan and allow to rest for 10 minutes, in a warm place. Stir any juices into the reserved pan juices with stock and heat, stirring to deglaze. Thicken with a roux of butter and flour, or gravy mix, and cook 2–3 minutes, then stir into a sauce dish. Cut a lid from inside top pastry ring to expose the meat, then carve the lamb with pastry and serve with the sauce and puréed spinach. *(Illustrated on page 74.)*

Mutton and Cabbage Pie

Serves: 6–8
Cooking time: 1–1¼ hours
Oven: 250°C 475°F

1 lb (500 g) lean mutton, diced
4 tablespoons flour
salt and pepper
½ teaspoon nutmeg
4 tablespoons butter
1 small onion, chopped
1 cup (250 ml) red wine
2 cups shredded cabbage
boiling salted water
Short Crust Pastry — see recipe page 86
1 egg, beaten with 2 teaspoons water
¼ cup (65 ml) hot Beef Stock — see recipe
page 90

Toss the diced mutton in a mixture of flour, salt, pepper and nutmeg. Melt butter in a flameproof casserole, add onion and sauté until golden, add meat and cook, stirring, until browned. Gradually stir in wine and bring to simmering point, cover and simmer gently for 35–40 minutes or until meat is tender. Meanwhile, cook the cabbage in a pan of boiling salted water for 8–10 minutes, drain well, add to the meat and stir, then set aside to cool.

Roll out ⅔ of the pastry dough on a floured board, line a greased 10″ (25 cm) fluted or quiche pan and add the cooled mixture. Roll out remaining dough and cover the pan, make a hole in the center and trim the pastry, then roll out a strip to fit around the edge of the pan. Brush egg glaze over the pastry, place strip in place, lightly crimp and glaze. Cook in a very hot oven for 15 minutes or until golden brown, remove pan from the oven, carefully pour hot stock into the pie through the hole and serve. *(Illustrated on page 74.)*

Lamb and Eggplant Casserole

Serves: 6
Cooking time: 1¼–1½ hours
Oven: 150°C 300°F

3 eggplants
salt
4 tablespoons oil
2 medium onions, chopped
1 clove garlic, crushed
2 tablespoons chopped parsley
½ teaspoon each of thyme, oregano and basil
salt and pepper
1 lb (500 g) lean lamb, minced
1 lb (500 g) ripe tomatoes, quartered
grated Parmesan cheese

Slice eggplants lengthways, place in a colander, sprinkle well with salt and leave for 1 hour to drain off the liquid. Heat 1 tablespoon oil in a large pan, add eggplant and cook for 5–6 minutes, turning to lightly brown, then lift out and drain.
Add 1 tablespoon of oil to pan juices and heat, add onions and sauté for 4–5 minutes, until golden. Add garlic, parsley, thyme, oregano, basil, salt, pepper and minced lamb and cook for 6–8 minutes, stirring, until meat is lightly browned.
Meanwhile, heat remaining oil in a separate pan, add tomatoes and cook, stirring, for 8–10 minutes.

until pulpy. Arrange layers of eggplant and meat in an ovenproof casserole dish, spoon tomato pulp around the edge of the dish and cook in a slow oven for 1 hour. Serve with grated Parmesan cheese.

Lamb Casserole with White Beans

Serves: 4–6
Cooking time: 2¼ hours

1 lb (500 g) white haricot beans
tepid water
salted water
1 small onion, stuck with 3–4 cloves
3 tablespoons butter
1 tablespoon oil
1½ lbs (750 g) lamb brisket, cubed
2 cloves garlic, crushed
*2 cups (500 ml) Beef Stock — see recipe
   page 90*
salt and pepper
½ teaspoon ground bay leaves
1 teaspoon thyme
4 tablespoons tomato purée
2 large tomatoes, peeled and chopped
finely chopped parsley
boiled rice

Soak the beans in a bowl of tepid water overnight, drain and place in a pan with salted water to cover, add onion stuck with cloves and bring to the boil, reduce heat, cover and simmer for 30 minutes, discard onion and drain.
Heat butter and oil in a flameproof casserole, add meat and cook over moderate heat until brown on all sides. Add garlic and stir, add stock, salt, pepper, ground bay leaves, thyme, tomato purée and drained beans and cover, bring to simmering point and simmer over low heat for 1 hour. Add tomatoes and cook a further 18–20 minutes, then serve, sprinkled with parsley, with hot rice.

Brains in Gherkin Onion Sauce

Serves: 4–6
Cooking time: 25–30 minutes

4 sets of lamb's brains, soaked, cooked and
   drained
6 tablespoons flour
salt and pepper
3 tablespoons butter
1 tablespoon oil
1 medium onion, chopped
½ cup (125 ml) white wine
½ cup (125 ml) Beef Stock — see recipe
   page 90
8–10 gherkins, finely chopped
¼ cup heavy cream

Cut prepared brains into quarters, toss in flour seasoned with salt and pepper and shake off excess, reserve seasoned flour. Heat butter and oil in a pan, add onion and sauté 2–3 minutes, add brains and cook, turning, until golden, then lift out brains and set aside. Add leftover seasoned flour to the pan and heat, stirring, until bubbly. Gradually stir in wine and stock and bring to simmering point. Return brains to the pan and baste, add gherkins, cover and simmer for 10–12 minutes, fold in cream and heat, but do not boil, then serve.

LAMB AND SAUERKRAUT WITH JUNIPER BERRIES (RECIPE PAGE 80) ▶

Lamb Chops in Sour Cream

Serves: 4
Cooking time: 1 hour

3 tablespoons oil
4–6 lamb chops, thickly cut
salt and pepper
dash of garlic salt
2 small carrots, sliced
1 medium onion, sliced
3 scallions, chopped
1 cup (250 ml) sour cream

Heat oil in a flameproof casserole, add lamb chops and cook until lightly browned, season with salt, pepper and garlic salt, add carrots and onion. Cover and simmer for 30 minutes, add scallions, cover and simmer a further 15 minutes. Remove chops and keep warm. Stir in sour cream and heat but do not boil, spoon over the chops and serve.

Lamb and Sauerkraut with Juniper Berries

Serves: 6–8
Cooking time: 1¾–2 hours
Oven: 230°C reduced to 180°C
       450°F reduced to 350°F

4 lbs (2 kg) lean leg of lamb
2 tablespoons juniper berries
4 tablespoons melted butter
¼ cup Vegetable Stock — see recipe page 90
4 tablespoons apple cider
salt and pepper
2 × 14 oz (440 g) cans sauerkraut
½ cup (125 ml) white wine
½ teaspoon sugar
salt to taste

Trim the lamb and cut incisions in the meat, insert 12 juniper berries and brush with melted butter, place in a baking pan and cook in a very hot oven for 15 minutes to seal and brown. Mix stock and cider together and pour over the lamb, reduce heat to moderate and cook for 30 minutes. Baste the meat and sprinkle with salt and pepper, add remaining juniper berries to the pan juices and cook a further 1–1¼ hours, basting occasionally. Meanwhile, mix sauerkraut and wine in a pan with sugar and salt to taste, cover and heat over low heat for 8–10 minutes. Lift out lamb to a serving dish, spoon sauerkraut around the meat, pour pan juices over both meat and sauerkraut and serve. (Illustrated on page 79.)

Italian Lamb Kebabs

Serves: 6
Cooking time: 18–20 minutes

2 lbs (1 kg) lean lamb, cubed
½ cup (125 ml) olive oil
½ cup (125 ml) Marsala or Madeira
1 tablespoon lemon juice
1 teaspoon oregano
1 clove garlic, crushed
½ teaspoon ground bay leaves
salt and pepper
1 green bell pepper, seeded and cut in chunks
3 medium onions, quartered

Place the lamb cubes in a glass or enamel dish. Combine oil, Marsala, lemon juice, oregano, garlic, ground bay leaves, salt and pepper in a jar, cover and shake vigorously until blended and creamy, then pour over the lamb, cover and set aside to marinate for 2 hours, basting occasionally. Lift out lamb cubes and drain, reserving marinade, thread on to skewers, alternately with green pepper chunks and onion quarters. Put kebabs on the broiler tray 4"–6" (10–15 cm) from heat and cook for 18–20 minutes, turning frequently and basting often with the marinade until meat is tender and brown, then serve.

Indonesian Lamb Curry

Serves: 6–8
Cooking time: 1¼ hours

4 tablespoons peanut oil
2 large onions, thinly sliced
3 cloves garlic, crushed
½ teaspoon cummin
2 teaspoons coriander
¼ teaspoon pepper
½ teaspoon cinnamon
¼ teaspoon ground cloves
½ teaspoon cardamom
1 teaspoon finely chopped ginger root
2 lbs (1 kg) lean lamb from the leg, diced
sprinkle of salt
3 cups (750 ml) coconut milk
1 tablespoon lemon juice
hot boiled rice
Lavash — see recipe page 88

Heat oil in a flameproof casserole, add onions and sauté until golden, add garlic and cook 1 minute. Add all the spices and stir well, then add diced lamb and salt, stir and cook over moderate heat for 5 minutes. Stir in coconut milk and bring to simmering point, stirring constantly, and simmer, uncovered, for 50–55 minutes, stirring occasionally until meat is tender. Stir in lemon juice and serve with hot rice, lavash and curry accompaniments. (See page 88.)

Chump Chops in Rosemary Marinade

Serves: 4
Cooking time: 12–15 minutes

4 tablespoons oil
2 tablespoons lemon juice
1 clove garlic, crushed
2 teaspoons rosemary
salt and pepper
8 chump chops 1" (2½ cm) thick

Combine oil, lemon juice, garlic, rosemary, salt and pepper in a jar, cover and shake well to mix for a marinade. Arrange chops in one layer in a shallow glass or enamel dish, pour marinade over the meat, baste and set aside in a cool place to marinate for 2 hours, basting occasionally. Lift out chops and place on the grill over medium hot coals and cook for 12–15 minutes, or cook 4"–6" (10–15 cm) from heat under the broiler until tender, turning often and basting with the marinade.

Lamb Chop Stew

Serves: 4
Cooking time: 1½–1¾ hours

4 tablespoons butter or margarine
1½ lbs (750 g) lamb chops
3 tablespoons flour
1 tablespoon curry powder
1 tablespoon tomato paste
1 tablespoon plum jam
1 cup (250 ml) white wine
1 cup (250 ml) water
salt and seasoned pepper
2 medium onions, sliced
2 medium carrots, sliced
1 medium parsnip, sliced
2 medium potatoes, peeled and sliced
boiled rice
chopped parsley

Melt butter or margarine in a flameproof casserole, add lamb chops and brown well on each side, remove chops and set aside. To pan juices add flour and curry powder and cook, stirring, until bubbly. Combine tomato paste, plum jam, wine, water, salt and seasoned pepper and mix until smooth, then stir into casserole and bring to the boil, stirring constantly. Return chops to the casserole, add onions, carrots, parsnips and potatoes and baste. Cover and simmer gently for 1¼–1½ hours until chops are tender. Serve with hot boiled rice and sprinkle with parsley.

Rotisserie of Rosemary Lamb

Serves: 4–6
Cooking time: 2–2¼ hours

4 lbs (2 kg) leg of lamb
2 cloves garlic, slivered
4 tablespoons dry breadcrumbs
1 tablespoon rosemary
1 tablespoon chopped parsley
1 extra clove garlic, crushed
salt and pepper
3 tablespoons melted butter
3 tablespoons lemon juice
¼ cup dry white wine
Sautéed Potatoes — see recipe page 35

Insert rotisserie rod through the center of the leg along the bone and secure with prongs, make slits in the meat and insert garlic slivers. Combine breadcrumbs, rosemary, parsley, crushed garlic, salt, pepper, melted butter and lemon juice in a bowl and mix well. Press this mixture onto the lamb on all sides, then set meat aside for 2 hours to absorb the flavors.

Place the rod in the oven rotisserie and cook at 190°C–375°F or mark 6 for 1¼ hours, baste with wine and cook a further 45–60 minutes or until tender, basting occasionally. Lift the meat to a carving dish, remove rod and let the lamb rest for 10 minutes in a warm place, then carve and serve with sautéed potatoes.

Sautéed Mushrooms

Serves: 2–4
Cooking time: 8–10 minutes

1 tablespoon butter
1 teaspoon oil
6 oz (185 g) mushrooms, sliced
1 scallion, white only, finely chopped
salt and pepper

Heat butter and oil in a pan until hot, add mushrooms and sauté 2–3 minutes, add scallion and sauté a further 2–3 minutes, season with salt and pepper and serve to accompany a dish for 2, or keep warm to add to a dish for 4.

Lemon Lamb

Serves: 4–6
Cooking time: 1½–1¾ hours
Oven: 180°C 350°F

4 lbs (2 kg) lean leg of lamb
2 cloves garlic, slivered
⅓ cup lemon juice
salt and pepper
1 teaspoon sweet basil
1 cup (250 ml) hot water
2 tablespoons melted butter

Cut slits in the lamb and insert slivers of garlic, brush the meat liberally with lemon juice and sprinkle with salt, pepper and basil. Place the lamb in a baking pan and cook in a moderate oven for 1 hour. Drain fat from the pan and add hot water, brush meat with melted butter and cook a further 30–40 minutes or until tender. Lift out lamb to a warm carving dish and allow to rest in a warm place for 10 minutes. Skim and discard fat from pan juices and reduce liquid a little over high heat, then pour into a sauce dish and serve with the lamb.

Sautéed Kidneys with Bacon

Serves: 4
Cooking time: 12–15 minutes

8 lamb's kidneys
1 cup (250 ml) milk
8 slices of lean bacon
2 tablespoons butter
salt and pepper
2 teaspoons Worcestershire sauce
few grains of cayenne pepper
finely chopped parsley

Trim kidneys, cut in half and discard skin and core, place in a bowl with milk and set aside to soak for 2 hours, then drain. Meanwhile, cook bacon slices until crisp, drain on paper towels and keep warm. Discard all but 2 tablespoons of drippings from pan, add butter and heat, add kidneys and cook over high heat to brown on all sides. Reduce heat, sprinkle with salt, pepper, sauce and cayenne, cover and simmer 3–4 minutes. Serve with bacon and sprinkle with parsley.

Mock Ham

Serves: 8–10
Cooking time: 3–3¼ hours

6–7 lbs (3 kg) corned leg of mutton or lamb
tepid water
8 whole cloves
1 tablespoon brown sugar
1 tablespoon malt vinegar
1 small onion, halved
a bouquet garni

Trim the mutton, rinse in cold water and place in a large pan, cover with tepid water and bring to the boil. Pour off water and refill to cover the meat with tepid water. Add cloves, brown sugar, vinegar, onion halves and a bouquet garni of thyme, bay leaf and parsley and bring to the boil. Reduce heat, cover and simmer gently for 3–3¼ hours, until meat is tender. Remove pan from heat and allow the meat to become cold. Lift out the leg, drain well, then wrap in plastic film and refrigerate.

Liver and Bacon

Serves: 4
Cooking time: 20–25 minutes

1 lamb's liver
6 tablespoons flour
salt and pepper
4 slices bacon, cut in half
1 cup (250 ml) water
3 teaspoons Worcestershire Sauce
finely chopped parsley

Remove the skin from the liver and cut into thin slices, discarding veins and tubes. Dredge in flour seasoned with salt and pepper and shake off excess; reserve seasoned flour.
Cook bacon in a large pan until crisp. Lift out, drain on paper towels and keep warm. Add liver to the pan juices and cook over moderate heat until brown and crisp, lift out, drain on paper towels and place with the bacon. Sprinkle leftover seasoned flour into the pan and cook 2–3 minutes to lightly brown. Gradually stir in water and Worcestershire sauce and bring to the boil, stirring and scraping to deglaze the pan. Cook 2–3 minutes, then serve over liver and bacon and sprinkle with parsley.

Stuffed Lamb Breasts on the Spit

Serves: 4–6
Cooking time: 1¼–1½ hours
Barbecue on the spit over medium hot coals

2 lamb breasts, boned and trimmed
Honey and Wine Marinade — see recipe
    page 91

Stuffing:
1 medium onion, finely chopped
1 teaspoon rosemary
4 slices ham, finely chopped
1 tablespoon finely chopped parsley
1½ cups cold, cooked rice
salt and seasoned pepper
¼ cup white wine

For the stuffing, combine all ingredients in a bowl and mix well.
Place the lamb breasts in a large dish and add marinade, baste and set aside for at least 2 hours, basting occasionally, then drain meat, reserving the marinade. Pat the meat dry and lay out on a board, skin side down. Portion the stuffing onto the breasts, roll firmly and fasten with skewers or tie with string. Thread spit rod through the center of each rolled breast and secure, place rod on the spit over medium hot coals and cook for 1¼–1½ hours or until tender, basting often with the reserved marinade in last 20–25 minutes, then serve.

Mediterranean Lamb Patties

Serves: 4–6
Cooking time: 18–20 minutes

1½ lb (750 g) lean lamb, ground
1 medium onion, minced
¼ lb (125 g) pine nuts
½ teaspoon nutmeg
salt and pepper
3 tablespoons oil
1 tablespoon Marsala or sherry
1 teaspoon chopped mint
pinch of thyme

In a bowl combine ground lamb, onion, pine nuts, nutmeg, salt and pepper and mix thoroughly. Add a little water if mixture is too dry, then shape into 8 patties. In a jar mix oil, Marsala, mint, thyme, salt and pepper, cover and shake well for a baste. Brush patties with the baste and place on the grill over hot coals and cook for 18–20 minutes, turning often and basting, or cook 4"–6" (10–15 cm) from heat under the broiler.

Liver and Grapes in Marsala

Serves: 4
Cooking time: 30–35 minutes

1½ lbs (750 g) lamb's liver
flour
salt and pepper
4 tablespoons butter
½ teaspoon oregano or marjoram
½ cup (125 ml) Beef Stock — see recipe
  page 90
¼ cup (65 ml) Marsala
½ lb (250 g) seedless white grapes
finely chopped parsley

Trim the liver, cut into thin slices and toss in flour seasoned with salt and pepper; reserve seasoned flour. Melt 2 tablespoons butter in a large pan until hot, add liver and cook until brown on all sides, then lift out and keep warm. Add remaining butter to the pan and heat, stir in 1 tablespoon of leftover seasoned flour and oregano and cook, stirring, until bubbling. Gradually stir in stock and Marsala and cook, stirring constantly, until thick and smooth. Return liver to the pan and baste, reduce heat, cover and simmer for 10–12 minutes. Add grapes, cover and simmer a further 4–5 minutes, then serve, sprinkled with chopped parsley.

Garlic and Herb Glazed Lamb

Serves: 4–6
Cooking time: 1–1¼ hours
Oven: 230°C reduced to 180°C
        450°F reduced to 350°F

2–3 lbs (1–1½ kg) boned leg of lamb
1 tablespoon melted butter
1 clove garlic, cut in half
¼ cup treacle
¼ cup red wine vinegar
2 cloves garlic, crushed
salt and seasoned pepper
2 tablespoons finely chopped parsley
grated rind of 1 lemon
½ cup (125 ml) water

Garlic and Herb Stuffing:
½ cup finely chopped parsley
1 teaspoon finely chopped fresh rosemary
3 scallions, finely chopped
¾ cup soft breadcrumbs
3 cloves garlic, crushed
½ teaspoon ground ginger
1 teaspoon salt
dash of pepper
¼ cup water

For the stuffing, combine all ingredients in a bowl and mix well.

Spread the lamb on a board, skin side down, and spread with the stuffing, roll to close and fasten with skewers or tie with string. Brush with melted butter and rub with cut garlic, place in a baking pan and cook in a very hot oven for 15 minutes to seal and brown, then reduce heat to moderate. Combine treacle, wine vinegar, crushed garlic, salt, seasoned pepper, parsley and lemon rind in a bowl and mix well, spread half the mixture over the lamb and cook for 45 minutes, basting in the last 20 minutes with pan juices. Remove meat to a carving dish and allow to rest for 10 minutes in a warm place. Pour off most of the fat in the pan, add water and heat, stirring and scraping to deglaze the pan, add remaining treacle, parsley mixture and bring to the boil, stirring, and simmer 2–3 minutes for a sauce. Carve the lamb and serve with the sauce spooned on top.

Lamb in Spicy Sauce

Serves: 6–8
Cooking time: 2–2¼ hours
Barbecue on the spit over medium hot coals

4 lbs (2 kg) boned leg of lamb
2 cups soft breadcrumbs
1 small onion, finely chopped
1 teaspoon rosemary
1 teaspoon mixed herbs
1 teaspoon chopped parsley
⅓ cup white wine
2 cloves garlic, halved
salt and pepper

Spicy Sauce:
4 tablespoons chutney
1 tablespoon Worcestershire sauce
1 tablespoon soy sauce
1 tablespoon tomato paste
3 tablespoons Marsala or sherry
2 tablespoons oil
pinch of cayenne pepper
1 tablespoon brown sugar

Trim meat, lay on a board, skin side down, and open up. Combine breadcrumbs, onion, rosemary, mixed herbs, parsley and wine in a bowl and mix well, then place mixture on meat, roll firmly and tie with string. Insert spit rod lengthways through the center of meat and secure, rub with garlic, sprinkle with salt and pepper and place on the spit over medium hot coals. Cook for 2–2¼ hours, until tender.
Meanwhile, combine all ingredients for sauce in a pan and mix well, then set on the side of the barbecue to warm. In last ½ hour of cooking, baste

the meat often with the sauce. Lift lamb from the spit on to a carving dish, remove rod and allow meat to rest for 10 minutes, then slice and serve with the remaining sauce.

Stuffed Crown Roast

Serves: 6
Cooking time: 1¼–1½ hours
Oven: 180°C   325°F

1 crown of 12 ribs
salt and pepper
1 tablespoon flour
1 cup (250 ml) Beef Stock — see recipe page 90
½ cup (125 ml) Marsala or sherry

Stuffing:
1 tablespoon butter
1 small onion, minced
1 clove garlic, crushed
¼ lb (125 g) sausage meat, ground
½ stalk celery, finely chopped
1½ cups soft breadcrumbs
1 tablespoon finely chopped fresh mint
1 tablespoon lemon juice
1 egg
salt and pepper

For the stuffing, melt butter in a pan, add onion and garlic and sauté 2–3 minutes, add sausage meat and cook, stirring, for 4–5 minutes to lightly brown. Remove pan from heat and add celery, breadcrumbs, mint, lemon juice, egg, salt and pepper and mix well.
Place the lamb crown in a baking pan and sprinkle with salt and pepper, spoon stuffing into the center and cover bone tips and stuffing with foil. Cook in a moderate oven for 1 hour, remove foil from the stuffing and cook a further 15–20 minutes or until tender. Using a slotted spoon, carefully lift the meat to a warm serving dish, and keep warm.
Pour off all but 2 tablespoons of drippings from pan, add flour and heat, stirring, until bubbly, add stock and cook, stirring and scraping to deglaze pan. Stir in Marsala and bring to the boil, stirring into a smooth sauce, then pour into a sauce dish. Replace foil on bone tips with paper frills and serve lamb with the sauce.

Oriental Shish-Kebabs

Serves: 6
Cooking time: 15–18 minutes

    3 lbs (1½ kg) boned lamb shoulder, cubed
    salt and pepper
    Honey and Wine Marinade — see recipe
        page 91
    12 small onions, peeled
    2 small green bell peppers, seeded and cut in
        chunks
    1 tablespoon brown sugar
    ½ cup (125 ml) tomato sauce
    2–3 drops Tabasco sauce

Sprinkle the lamb cubes with salt and pepper and place in a glass dish, add marinade and baste well, cover and chill overnight. Lift out meat, reserving marinade, and thread on skewers, alternating with onions and green pepper chunks, and cook under a broiler for 15–18 minutes, turning often. Meanwhile, in a pan combine reserved marinade with brown sugar, tomato and Tabasco sauces and heat to simmering, then serve over the shish-kebabs.

Marinated Kebabs with Onions and Bacon

Serves: 6
Cooking time: 18–20 minutes

    2 lbs (1 kg) lean lamb, cubed
    ¼ cup tomato sauce
    ¼ cup thick fruit chutney
    1 tablespoon vinegar
    1 tablespoon soy sauce
    1 tablespoon oil
    1 tablespoon firmly packed brown sugar
    3 medium onions, cut in wedges
    3 bacon slices, cut into pieces

Place lamb cubes in a glass or enamel dish. Combine tomato sauce, fruit chutney, vinegar, soy sauce, oil and brown sugar in a bowl and mix well, then pour over the lamb and stir to coat all the meat

cubes. Cover and chill for at least 2 hours. Lift lamb from the marinade and thread on skewers, alternately with onion wedges and bacon pieces and cook under a pre-heated broiler, 4"–6" (10–15 cm) from heat for 18–20 minutes, turning often and basting with the marinade, then serve.

Fritter Batter

Makes almost 2 cups

    1 cup plain flour
    pinch of salt
    1 whole egg
    1 egg, separated
    1¼ cups (300 ml) milk, water or mixture of the
        two
    1 tablespoon melted butter
    2 tablespoons oil

Sift flour and salt into a bowl and make a deep well in the center. Beat whole egg, egg yolk and milk together and pour into the well. Gradually beat in flour until blended, beat in melted butter and oil until smooth and creamy, then set bowl aside for at least 2 hours. Beat egg white and fold into the batter.

Short Crust Pastry

    ½ lb (2 cups) self-raising flour
    3 teaspoons cornstarch
    pinch of salt
    ⅓ cup (85 g) butter
    3 tablespoons lard
    1 egg, lightly beaten
    juice of 1 lemon
    cold water

Sift flour, cornstarch and salt together into a bowl, add butter and lard and rub in with the fingertips, lifting hands to aerate the mixture, until crumbly. Mix in egg and lemon juice and add only enough water to make a stiff dough. Turn dough out on to a floured board and knead lightly, roll into a ball, wrap and chill until required.

Fresh Relish

Makes about 2 cups
Cooking time: 12–15 minutes

2 large tomatoes, peeled and chopped
1 large onion, chopped
2 stalks of celery with leaves, chopped
1 large apple, peeled, cored and chopped
½ small red bell pepper, seeded and chopped
1 clove garlic, crushed
1 teaspoon salt
1 tablespoon chopped parsley
2 tablespoons firmly packed brown sugar
3 tablespoons red wine vinegar
small pinch seasoned pepper
½ teaspoon thyme

Combine all ingredients in a pan and bring to simmering point, cover and simmer for 10–12 minutes. Cool, put through a blender to purée and return to a bowl. Cover and chill until required. Serve hot or cold with broiled or barbecued lamb or cold lamb salad.

Wine Court-bouillon

Makes about 4 cups
Cooking time: 30 minutes

2 cups (500 ml) water
2 cups (500 ml) white wine
2 teaspoons salt
1 small carrot, chopped
1 medium onion, chopped
6 peppercorns, bruised
2 whole cloves
1 bay leaf
½ stalk celery with leaves, chopped
2 sprigs fresh parsley
1 teaspoon thyme

Combine all ingredients in a deep pan and bring to simmering point, cover and simmer for 30 minutes. Strain through a fine sieve into a bowl and cool, cover and chill until required.

Basic Bouillon

Makes about 6 cups (1½ liters)
Cooking time: 4–4½ hours

1½ lbs (750 g) shin of beef
1 chicken carcass
1 small onion
1 small carrot
1 tablespoon butter
2 teaspoons salt
½ stalk celery, chopped
1 tablespoon chopped parsley
1 teaspoon ground bay leaves
1 teaspoon thyme
4–5 peppercorns, bruised
10 cups (2½ liters) water

Chop the beef, break up the chicken carcass and slice onion and carrot thickly. Place beef and chicken in a deep pan with butter and cook over moderate heat for 10–12 minutes, stirring often. Add onion and carrot and cook a further 8–10 minutes. Add salt, celery, parsley, ground bay leaves, thyme, peppercorns and water, bring to the boil and simmer, uncovered, for 3½–4 hours, or until liquid is reduced by almost one third. Strain through muslin and a sieve into a bowl and cool, chill, then discard any fat on the surface.

Mint Sauce

Makes about ¾ cup

4–5 large sprigs of mint
4 tablespoons malt vinegar
3 tablespoons sugar
½ cup (125 ml) boiling water

Rinse the mint under running cold water and shake off excess. Tear off leaves and place in a blender, add vinegar, wait one moment, then add sugar and boiling water. Whirl on medium speed for 2 minutes, until blended. Pour into a sauce dish and cool before serving.

Curry Accompaniments

BANANAS IN YOGURT SAUCE:

Makes about 2½ cups

2 tablespoons lemon juice
¾ cup (185 ml) plain yogurt
1 teaspoon sugar
small pinch of salt
small pinch of chili powder
3 large bananas, peeled and thinly sliced
1 teaspoon hot melted butter
1 teaspoon cumin

Combine lemon juice, yogurt, sugar, salt and chili powder in a bowl and mix until blended. Place banana slices in a glass bowl, add yogurt mixture and toss gently, but thoroughly. Mix hot melted butter and cumin together, pour over the bananas and toss gently, cover and chill until required.

LAVASH:

Makes about 16
Cooking time: 20–25 minutes
Oven: 200°C 400°F

2¾ cups flour
¼ cup sugar
½ teaspoon salt
½ teaspoon bicarbonate of soda
½ cup (125 g) butter or margarine
1 cup (250 ml) buttermilk
toasted poppy or sesame seeds

Sift flour, sugar, salt and soda into a bowl, rub in butter or margarine until mixture holds together. Add buttermilk and poppy or sesame seeds, mix and form into walnut size balls, roll out balls on a floured surface until paper thin. Place 4 at a time on an ungreased oven tray and cook in a hot oven for 5 minutes or until lightly browned. Cool on a wire rack, store in an airtight container and serve with curry.

TOMATOES AND SCALLIONS IN MINT SAUCE:

Makes about 2 cups

4 medium tomatoes, peeled and chopped
6 scallions, white only, finely sliced
3 tablespoons minced fresh mint
3 tablespoons lemon juice
⅛ teaspoon salt
2 teaspoons sugar
¼ teaspoon chili powder

Place tomatoes and scallions in a glass bowl. Combine mint, lemon juice, salt, sugar and chili powder in a jar, cover and shake briskly until blended. Pour over tomatoes and scallions and gently toss, cover and chill overnight.

FRESH TOMATO CHUTNEY:

Makes about 1½ cups

1 large tomato, peeled and finely chopped
½ stalk celery, finely chopped
2 spring onions, bulbs only, chopped
1 teaspoon chili powder
3 tablespoons salad oil
2 teaspoons vinegar

Combine all ingredients in a bowl and mix well, cover and chill until required.

MINT AND SCALLION PURÉE:

Makes about 1¾ cups

1 cup minced mint leaves
4 scallions, white only, minced
¼ teaspoon chili sauce
2 tablespoons water
1 teaspoons sugar
2 teaspoons sugar
¼ cup lemon juice

Combine all ingredients in a blender and whirl until a smooth purée, spoon into a jar, cover and chill until required.

APPLES IN COCONUT:

Makes about 2½ cups

> 2 cooking apples, peeled, cored and diced
> 1 tablespoon lemon juice
> 1 small onion, minced
> ¼ cup minced green bell pepper
> salt
> 4 tablespoons shredded coconut
> 2 tablespoons hot milk

Place diced apples in a glass bowl and sprinkle with lemon juice, add minced onion, green pepper and salt to taste. Soak coconut in hot milk for 10–12 minutes or until cool, then add to the apples, stir well, cover and chill.

ONIONS WITH CHILI SAUCE:

Makes about ¾ cup

> ½ teaspoon chili powder
> salt and pepper
> 4 tablespoons lemon juice
> 2 medium white onions, thinly sliced

Combine chili powder, salt, pepper and lemon juice in a jar, cover and shake briskly to blend, add onion slices and gently shake, then chill overnight.

MINT AND GARLIC PURÉE:

Makes almost ½ cup

> 4 tablespoons minced mint
> 2 cloves garlic, crushed
> ½ teaspoon sugar
> ½ teaspoon chili powder
> 1 tablespoon vinegar

Combine all ingredients in a blender and mix until a smooth purée, spoon into a small bowl, cover and chill.

CUCUMBER IN YOGURT SAUCE:

Makes about 1½ cups

> 1 large cucumber, peeled, and thinly sliced
> salt
> 1 clove garlic, crushed
> ¼ teaspoon minced ginger root
> ¾ cup (185 ml) plain yogurt
> pinch of extra salt
> 1 teaspoon finely chopped chives

Place cucumber in a bowl and sprinkle with salt, cover and chill for at least 1 hour and drain in a colander, rinse under running water and drain again, pressing to remove all liquid, then return to a clean bowl. Combine garlic, ginger, yogurt, extra salt and chives in a bowl and mix well, pour over the cucumber and stir, cover and chill until required.

APPLE, GREEN PEPPER AND RAISIN PURÉE:

Makes about 1½ cups

> 2 cooking apples, peeled, cored and finely
>   chopped
> 2 tablespoons lemon juice
> 2 medium green bell peppers, seeded and finely
>   chopped
> 2 tablespoons chopped seedless raisins
> ⅛ teaspoon paprika
> ⅛ teaspoon cayenne pepper
> ¼ teaspoon salt
> 1 teaspoon sugar

Combine all ingredients in a blender and mix until a smooth purée, spoon into a jar, cover and chill until required.

OTHER CURRY ACCOMPANIMENTS:

Banana slices tossed in lemon juice
Crisp fried bacon, crumbled
Grated fresh coconut
Hard boiled eggs riced through a coarse sieve
Paratha — tortillas cooked in oil
Pappadams — spiced Indian bread

Beef Stock

Makes about 10 cups (2½ liters)
Cooking time: 2½–2¾ hours

2 lbs (1 kg) shin of beef or gravy beef, chopped
10 cups (2½ liters) cold water
2 teaspoons salt
a bouquet garni
1 medium onion, stuck with 3–4 cloves
½ stalk celery with leaves, chopped
1 medium carrot, chopped

Place meat in a large, deep pan with cold water and salt and very slowly bring to the boil, skim off the top and reduce heat. Add a bouquet garni of bay leaf, parsley and thyme, onion stuck with cloves, celery and carrot, cover and simmer gently for 2½ hours. Skim well, then pour through muslin and a fine sieve into a bowl, cool and chill. Carefully scoop off and discard the layer of fat, cover, and chill stock until required.

Chicken Stock

Makes about 10 cups (2½ liters)
Cooking time: 2½–2¾ hours

3 lbs (1½ kg) chicken
10 cups (2½ liters) cold water
1 teaspoon salt
4–5 peppercorns, bruised
1 bay leaf, crumbled
1 tablespoon chopped parsley
½ teaspoon thyme
1 medium onion, stuck with 3–4 cloves
1 medium carrot, sliced
1 stalk of celery with leaves, roughly chopped
1 clove garlic, halved
2 leeks, sliced

Place chicken in a large deep pan with water, salt and peppercorns. Tie crumbled bay leaf, parsley and thyme in a muslin bag (or use commercial bouquet garni) and add to the pan with onion stuck with cloves, carrot, celery, garlic and leeks and bring slowly to the boil, then reduce heat and skim the surface, cover tightly and simmer for 55–60 minutes or until chicken is tender. Skim the surface and carefully lift out chicken, tear off all the flesh and reserve for a separate dish. Chop the carcass, return to the pan with the bones and continue simmering a further 1½ hours. Skim the surface well, then strain through muslin and a fine sieve into a bowl. Cool and chill, then carefully remove and discard the layer of fat. Cover and chill until stock is required.

Vegetable Stock

Makes about 10 cups (2½ liters)
Cooking time: 3–3¼ hours

2 large onions
2 large carrots
1 stalk and leaves of celery
1 very small turnip
2 tablespoons butter
1 tablespoon chopped parsley
2 bay leaves, crumbled
1 teaspoon thyme
4–5 peppercorns, bruised
2 teaspoons salt
15 cups (3¾ liters) hot water
1 beef bouillon cube

Wash, peel and chop the vegetables. Melt butter in a deep pan, add onions and sauté for 4–5 minutes until lightly browned, add carrots, celery and turnip and cook over low heat, stirring to lightly brown. Tie parsley, bay leaves and thyme in muslin for a bouquet garni and add to the pan with peppercorns, salt, bouillon cube, and hot water. Bring to the boil, then reduce heat, half cover the pan and simmer for 2¾–3 hours, until liquid is reduced by a third. Strain through a fine sieve into a large bowl, cool, then chill. When cold, remove any fat. Cover and store in refrigerator until required.

Hot Water Mayonnaise

Makes almost 1½ cups

2 egg yolks
salt and pepper
1 teaspoon French mustard
1 tablespoon boiling water
1¼ cups (300 ml) olive oil
1½ tablespoons white vinegar

Put egg yolks, salt, pepper and mustard in a blender and mix on speed 3 for 2 minutes, add boiling water and blend for 1–2 minutes. Still blending, add the oil in a steady stream through the hole in the lid insert. Continue blending until the mixture is thick, then add vinegar and blend 2 minutes.

Mint Marinade and Baste

Makes almost ⅔ cup

2 tablespoons finely chopped fresh mint
½ teaspoon thyme
salt and pepper
⅓ cup oil
¼ cup dry white wine

Combine all ingredients in a blender and blend until mixed thoroughly and smooth. Pour into a jar, cover and chill until required. Shake briskly before using.

Herb Baste

Makes a little over ¾ cup

½ cup (125 ml) salad oil
1 small onion, finely chopped
1 clove garlic, crushed
1 teaspoon thyme
1 teaspoon marjoram
1 teaspoon salt
dash of seasoned pepper
3 tablespoons chopped parsley
3 tablespoons lemon juice

Combine all ingredients in a blender and mix until smooth, pour into a jar and set aside for at least 2 hours for flavors to fully mingle. Shake well before using.

Spicy Honey Baste

Makes almost 1 cup

¼ teaspoon prepared hot mustard
2 tablespoons white wine
salt and pepper
2 tablespoons honey
2 drops Tabasco sauce
1 teaspoon Worcestershire Sauce
1 tablespoon lemon juice
½ cup (125 ml) olive oil

Mix mustard with wine in a jar until smooth, add remaining ingredients, cover and shake briskly, or put through a blender until blended and smooth. Keep chilled until required.

Honey and Wine Marinade

Makes about ¾ cup
Cooking time: 6–8 minutes

1 clove garlic, crushed
½ teaspoon finely chopped tarragon
2 teaspoons finely chopped mint
2 tablespoons honey
1 tablespoon olive oil
½ cup (125 ml) white wine

Combine garlic, tarragon and mint in a pan with honey, olive oil and wine, bring to simmering point and simmer 5–6 minutes. Remove from heat and set aside for 1 hour to cool and allow flavors to blend. Pour into a jar, cover and chill until required.

Brown Butter Sauce

Makes about 1¼ cups
Cooking time: 10–12 minutes

¾ cup (185 g) butter
3 tablespoons finely chopped parsley
4 tablespoons lemon juice
salt and pepper to taste

Heat the butter in a pan until foamy, skim off the foam and pour clear yellow liquid through a fine sieve into a separate pan for clarified butter. Heat until golden brown, but not dark. Remove pan from heat, add parsley, stir and pour into a bowl over a pan of simmering water. Stir lemon juice into the same pan with salt and pepper and cook over high heat to reduce by ⅓. Stir into the bowl and keep warm over hot water until ready to use. Serve with roast lamb or grilled chops.

Béchamel Sauce

Makes about 1½ cups
Cooking time: 12–15 minutes

1¼ cups (300 ml) milk
1 bay leaf
small pinch of mace
1 small onion, minced
pinch of salt
3 peppercorns, bruised
1 tablespoon butter
1 tablespoon flour
2 tablespoons cream, whipped

Combine milk, bay leaf, mace, onion, salt and peppercorns in a pan, cover and heat very slowly for 7–8 minutes until warm, to infuse. Strain milk into a bowl and set aside.
Melt butter in a pan, add flour and stir to a roux and cook, stirring, 1–2 minutes. Remove pan from heat and add strained milk, then beat briskly until blended and smooth. Return pan to heat and bring to the boil, stirring constantly, reduce heat and simmer 2–3 minutes. Fold in whipped cream and stir until smooth.

Marion's Sauce

Makes about 1½ cups
Cooking time: 4–5 minutes

6 scallions, minced
grated rind from 1 orange
grated rind from 1 lemon
water
⅓ cup orange juice
2 tablespoons lemon juice
¼ teaspoon prepared hot mustard
pinch of ground ginger
pinch of cayenne pepper
½ cup (125 ml) warmed red currant jam
½ cup (125 ml) Madeira or sherry

Combine scallions with grated orange and lemon rind in a pan, cover with water and cook for 4–5 minutes, drain well and place in a bowl with orange and lemon juices, mustard, ginger and cayenne and stir to mix well. Stir in warmed jam and Madeira and mix until smooth, cover and chill. Serve with hot or cold meats, particularly lamb or mutton.

Herb Vinaigrette

Makes a little over 1 cup

¼ cup malt vinegar
¾ cup (185 ml) olive oil
¾ teaspoon prepared hot mustard
1 tablespoon finely chopped parsley
½ teaspoon finely chopped rosemary
1 teaspoon finely chopped tarragon
1 teaspoon finely chopped chervil
2 teaspoons finely chopped chives
¾ teaspoon salt
2 ice cubes (2 teaspoons each)

Combine all ingredients in a blender and whirl until mixture is thick, creamy and fully blended. Pour into a jar, cover and refrigerate until required.

Liquid Measures Table

IMPERIAL	METRIC
1 teaspoon	5 ml
*1 tablespoon (Aust)	20 ml
2 fluid ounces (¼ cup)	65 ml
4 fluid ounces (½ cup)	125 ml
8 fluid ounces (1 cup)	250 ml
1 pint (20 fluid ounces = 2½ cups)	625 ml

USA	METRIC
*1 tablespoon (also UK and NZ)	15 ml
1 pint (16 ounces = 2 cups)	500 ml
All other measures same as	
for imperial, above	

*Tablespoon measures used in the recipes in this book are 15 ml.

Solid Measures Table

AVOIRDUPOIS	METRIC
1 ounce	30 g
4 ounces (¼ lb)	125 g
8 ounces (½ lb)	250 g
12 ounces (¾ lb)	375 g
16 ounces (1 lb)	500 g
24 ounces (1½ lb)	750 g
32 ounces (2 lb)	1000 g (1 kg)

Oven Temperature Table

DESCRIPTION	GAS		ELECTRIC		DIAL MARK
	C	F	C	F	
Cool	100	200	110	225	¼
Very slow	120	250	120	250	½
Slow	150	300	150	300	1−2
Moderately slow	160	325	170	340	3
Moderate	180	350	190	375	4
Moderately hot	190	375	220	425	5−6
Hot	200	400	250	475	6−7
Very hot	230	450	270	525	8−9

Index

Notes